clothing

compass

Christian Explorations of Daily Living

David H. Jensen, Series Editor

Playing
James H. Evans Jr.

Shopping
Michelle A. Gonzalez

Eating and Drinking
Elizabeth T. Groppe

Dreaming
Barbara A. Holmes

Parenting
David H. Jensen

Working
Darby Kathleen Ray

Traveling
Joerg Rieger

Clothing
Michele Saracino

clothing

Michele Saracino

Fortress Press

Minneapolis

CLOTHING
Compass Series
Christian Explorations of Daily Living

Unless otherwise noted, scripture quotations are the author's own translation or from the New Revised Standard Version Bible, copyright © 1989 by the Division of Christian Education of the National Council of Churches of Christ in the USA, and are used with permission.

Cover design: Laurie Ingram
Book design: Christy J. P. Barker

Library of Congress Cataloging-in-Publication Data
Saracino, Michele, 1971–
   Clothing / Michele Saracino.
      p. cm. — (Compass series, Christian explorations of daily living)
   Includes bibliographical references.
ISBN 978-0-8006-9906-2 (pbk.: alk. paper) — ISBN 978-1-4514-2441-6 (ebook)
1. Clothing and dress—Moral and ethical aspects. 2. Clothing and dress—Religious aspects—Christianity. I. Title.
   BJ1697.S27 2012
   241'.674—dc23
                              2012008044

The paper used in this publication meets the minimum requirements of American National Standard for Information Sciences—Permanence of Paper for Printed Library Materials, ANSI Z329.48-1984.

Manufactured in the U.S.A.
16 15 14 13 12 1 2 3 4 5 6 7 8 9 10

contents

series foreword

Everyday practices matter for Christian faith. Our ordinary routines—eating, cooking, working, walking, shopping, playing, and parenting—are responses to the life God gives to the world. Christian faith claims that the ordinary materials and practices of human life are graced by God's presence: basic foodstuffs become the Body of Christ in a shared meal, water becomes the promise of new birth as ordinary people gather in Christ's name, and a transformed household becomes a metaphor for God's reign. Bodies, baths, meals, and households matter to Christian faith because God takes these everyday practices and materials as God's own: blessing, redeeming, and transforming them so that they more nearly reflect the hope and grace that come to us in the midst of the everyday. Christian faith does not flee from the everyday but embeds itself in daily, ordinary routines. This book series considers everyday practices as sites for theological reflection. When we pay close attention to everyday practices, we can glimpse classical Christian themes—redemption, creation, and incarnation—in new light. This book series does not attempt to *apply* classical doctrines to particular practices, but to offer narratives of ordinary routines, explore how immersion in them affects Christian life in a global world, and imagine how practice might re-form theology and theology re-form practice.

The series also explores the implications of globalization for daily practices and how these ordinary routines are implicated—for good and for ill—in the often bewildering effects of an increasingly interconnected world. Everyday practices, after all, are the places where the global becomes local. We encounter globalization not in abstract theory, but in the routine affairs of shopping at the corner grocery for food grown on the other side of the globe, maintaining friendships with persons on other continents, and in jobs where workplace decisions ripple outward to seemingly distant neighbors. Daily practices put a human face on the complex phenomenon of globalization and offer one place to begin theological reflection on this phenomenon. Paying close attention to these practices helps unveil the injustice as well as the hope of a global world. Since unreflective and consumptive forms of these daily practices often manifest themselves in American consumer society, this series also offers concrete suggestions for how daily practices might be reconfigured to more nearly reflect the hope and justice that is given to the world by God's grace. If daily practices implicate our complicity in global injustice, they might also be sites to imagine that world alternatively.

Though each book displays an organization uniquely its own, every title in the series offers three common themes: (1) The books offer thick descriptions of particular practices in North American society. What do parenting, cooking, and dressing look like in American communities in the twenty-first century? (2) The books survey varied Christian understandings of each practice, summoning theological resources for enhanced understanding and critique of typical forms of practice. What have Christians said about eating, dreaming, and traveling throughout their history, and how do their reflections matter today? (3) The books offer a constructive restatement of each practice and explore how ordinary practices might reshape or sharpen beliefs and themes of Christian faith. How does attention to practice affect the way we understand Christian theology, and how does attention to theology affect the way we understand everyday practice? Each book shares the conviction that Christian life is best encountered (and often best understood) in the midst of the ordinary.

Many of the authors of each volume are members of the Workgroup in Constructive Theology, an ecumenical group of teachers and scholars that writes and teaches theology in dialogue with contemporary critiques of Christian traditions. We are diverse in theological and denominational orientation yet share the recognition that Christian theology has often been employed for abusive ends. Theological traditions have silenced women, people of color, the poor, and GLBT persons. Our constructive restatements of Christian practice, therefore, do not simply restate classical Christian traditions, but question them as we learn from them. We listen to the past while we also critique it, just as we hope that subsequent generations will also criticize and learn from us. Because so many voices have been silenced throughout the church's history, it is essential that Christian theologians attend to voices beyond the corridors of ecclesial and social power. Outside these corridors, after all, is where Christian faith takes root in ordinary life. Though each of us writes theology somewhat differently—some with explicit schools of theology in mind, such as liberationist or womanist theology—we all share the conviction that theology *matters*, not simply for reflective life, but for the life of the world. Christian theology, at its best, is one expression of life's fullness and flourishing. Our words, in other words, ought to point to a more abundant life of grace in the face of the death-dealing forces at work on an economically stratified and ecologically threatened planet.

We have written these books with a minimum of technical jargon, intending them to be read in a wide variety of settings. The books may be used in seminary and undergraduate courses, including introductions to theology, ethics, and Christian spirituality. Clergy will also find them useful as they seek brief, yet substantive, books on Christian life that will inform their work of preaching, counseling, and teaching. We also imagine that each text could be used in churches for adult education classes. Many Christians seek guides for how faith is lived but are disenchanted with conservative approaches that shun dialogue with the wider culture of religious diversity. This series offers a progressive, culturally engaged approach to daily practices, globalization, and Christian theology. We think the books are as important in the questions they ask as in the answers they attempt.

David H. Jensen
Austin Presbyterian Theological Seminary

preface

Human beings, like all mammals, are born into the world without clothing. But unlike other mammals, we are swaddled in clothes from the moment of our birth and spend most of the rest of our lives in various forms of dress. We get dressed for many reasons: to protect ourselves from elements such as cold weather and sun, to cover up parts of the body out of modesty, to express ourselves in colors and styles, to follow trends and external standards of beauty and fashion. Clothing is both a basic necessity *and* an expression of the human spirit. What we wear conveys our creativity *and* our conformity to ideals and standards we did not create. Though we may not accept the mantra that "clothes make the person," our dress often does reveal much about ourselves. Some of us may pay more attention to what we wear than others, but all of us are affected and shaped by practices of dress and adornment. Many of us, however, have not considered clothing to be a practice of faith.

In this elegant and accessible book, Michele Saracino urges us to think otherwise. Practices of dress have much to contribute to Christian faith (and vice versa). Saracino urges us to examine more closely the customs that govern what we wear and consider more directly the places where our clothing is made and the people who weave and knit its fabrics. She begins by considering the "mirror moments" that begin our days, the questions we pose to ourselves as we get dressed. By attending to these moments and our responses to them, she reframes some fundamental themes of human personhood in the Christian tradition: vulnerability and relatedness, sin and redemption, anxiety and hope. Along the way, she also suggests that the incarnation—Word becoming flesh and dwelling among us—is a form of dress. In the flesh of Jesus, we see that clothing is meant not so much to cover up as to make us vulnerable and open to one another. And that recognition causes us to see all things clothed anew.

David H. Jensen

introduction: the mirror moment

Perhaps you have had one of these mornings, when you find yourself standing in front of your mirror, drowning in a pile of tangled clothes. Every item of clothing you have put on makes you feel bad about yourself and your entire existence. As you toss the clothes to the ground you begin to panic, wondering if you are ever going to find something to wear and if you are ever going to get to work on time. As the shirts, skirts, pants, and jackets accumulate, you fear that you will be swallowed up by them and all the negative feelings they have created. At a moment such as this, what stings more than any disapproving word from a parent, teacher, or friend is seeing in the mirror the disappointed eyes of your worst critic—you! The power of dress is astonishing. The day before, you might have felt great about your life and future; now, as you gaze at your reflection, all your hopes and dreams have vanished.

If this is or ever has been your story, you are, like me, one of the lucky ones. Amid the inequities of the global landscape, I am profoundly privileged to own a bounty of clothes from which to "choose," made from a variety of fabrics that keep me warm in the icy winters and cool in the hot summers. But acknowledging this only makes me feel worse about myself, by compelling me to reflect on

1

my vague awareness of the social inequities in the clothing industry. I teach at a liberal arts college, and in my line of work thinking is never bad, yet the questions triggered by my standing in front of the mirror overwhelm me. Along with questioning why I feel social pressure to wear this or that dress, I wonder how my dress was produced, at what cost, and to whom. In this mirror moment, I begin to wonder about the young bodies that were worn out in making my clothes—bodies that can never wear such clothing because of its high cost. Juggling all these thoughts and feelings in my head, I am completely undone by seven o'clock in the morning.

Exposing my feelings and private struggles with dress makes me cringe in embarrassment. I am well aware that I risk appearing to be vain and superficial or, even worse, being seen as a privileged person who does not want to feel guilty. Being vain seems to be tolerable—practically a virtue—in our day and age, if the end result is looking good and hence feeling better. On the other hand, being guilt-ridden is often understood as a curse in that it holds one back from accomplishing all the things they need and want to do. Whatever the case, in the midst of my vanity and guilt, I have come to realize from sharing these mirror moments that I am not alone. In one of my favorite courses to teach, called Religion and the Body, we discuss how our daily rituals—such as eating, exercising, and dressing—have religious significance. The students

> Muddling through that pile of clothes might be considered one version of what Christians call the fall, original sin, or the brokenness that complicates human existence.

practically end up instructing the class themselves because they have so many experiences with these practices, all of which are connected to being vulnerable. Hearing my students' testimonies, I am convinced that everyday happenings related to what we wear and why we wear it offer insights into the complex journey of being a creature in the world with God and others.

From a Christian perspective, our ordinary daily routines reveal and call into question fundamental convictions about what it means to be vulnerable, to be free, and to be obligated to others. Referring again to "the mirror moment," muddling through that pile of clothes might be considered one version of what Christians call the fall, original sin, or the brokenness that complicates human existence. If Christians believe we are born into patterns of daily living that restrict our freedom and the freedom of others—patterns that, if unchecked, could lead to emotional and physical pain and suffering—then reflecting on mirror moments is neither superficial nor self-indulgent. Rather, it is potentially transformative, moving us toward life-giving relations with God and others.

Clothing as Spiritual

In my Religion and the Body course, when we begin the unit on dress, students are all too happy to share their experiences of attending parochial schools and being forced into conformance with particular dress codes. Female students describe how they would defy the school rules by rolling up their skirts, and male students lament their feelings of powerlessness against the anonymity they experienced when wearing their uniforms. These examples often generate a lively debate about the differences between attending private and public schools, focusing on which type of institution grants students more freedom to be themselves. Amazingly, students who have not yet spoken a word in class are unable to stop sharing and reflecting on their experiences. While some who attended public schools guess that they would have resented the lack of freedom to dress the way they chose, others who attended private schools are nostalgic for dress codes and miss their uniforms. Students who liked uniforms believe that the freedom from daily decisions about what they should wear and why they should wear it allowed them to be more themselves in school. It becomes clear that students crave freedom, creativity, safety, peace, and beauty in their dress, and depending on the individuals and their circumstances, some practices are more life-giving than others. Unbeknownst to themselves, through their storytelling, these students are working toward their own spirituality of dress. Most impressively, in the course of lively and honest conversation, they begin the process of what I like to call "getting naked," that is, telling one's stories and being vulnerable with others.

> When a loved one dies, we treasure articles of the person's clothing; we hold shirts close to remember the loved one's perfume and wear his or her jackets to feel the person with us. These pieces of our loved one's stories are as valuable to us as any relic of a saint.

What my students prove during class discussion, time and time again, is that in many ways, the spiritual import of dress is already part of our everyday life. We just don't articulate it as such, for any number of reasons, including a lack of time or interest. Without a verbal narration, our clothes tell our stories. When a loved one dies, we treasure articles of the person's clothing; we hold shirts close to remember the loved one's perfume and wear his or her jackets to feel the person with us. These pieces of our loved one's stories are as valuable to us as any relic of a saint. The way we dress also has spiritual import because it stands as our testimony to the world, witnessing to who we are and what our values reflect. As we do in prayer and in celebration of the sacraments, when we dress, we express our hope for life-giving relationships, love, peace, and acceptance.

Playing the Devil's Advocate

Some may want to question the feasibility of a spirituality of dress, skeptical of whether clothing and religion really relate. While some instances of dress clearly connect with religious issues, others are less obvious. Muslim women who veil, Roman Catholic nuns who wear habits, and Mormons who wear undergarments are all engaged in religiously charged dress practices that are clearly worthy of analysis. In the following pages, I am asking readers to consider these issues and more. Specifically, I am concerned with how—beyond reading the symbolic meaning of a single article of clothing, such as a clerical collar or a cross on a necklace—it is important to reflect on how our rituals and processes of dress tell our stories and reveal our anxieties about being a creature in relation to God and others.

Even if we agree that the topic of what we wear and why we wear it is interesting, and even if we can find examples and stories about dress as spiritual, the question still arises as to whether this topic is terribly profound. Aren't war and poverty more important issues for Christians to deal with than fashion and popular culture? The fashion industry, while creative, lucrative, and exciting, is still an industry—a term that itself cultivates suspicion and contempt. This is not to say that any and all industries are evil, just that they are driven by profit—an end goal that does not always foster life-giving relations. It seems strange to talk about God and grace in the shadow of celebrity, where we hear constant chatter about this or that latest fashion, this or that latest diet fad, and this or that failed relationship or scandal. How can spirituality unfold in such a hollow, despair-filled world? What I attempt to demonstrate in this book is that in the midst of this ambivalence over the fashion industry, Christians are called to embrace our clothing practices as spiritual. It is precisely here on the ground or in front of the mirror where meaningful work about Christian interpretations of the human person begins.

An even more daunting obstacle to admitting the relevance of dress to philosophical and theological inquiry is what some call "the body problem"—the assumption that anything related to our physical natures and daily routines is less important than our rational endeavors. The body problem is rooted in the age-old denial of the significance of flesh and feeling and their interconnection with thought processes. From Plato to Paul, from Augustine to Aquinas, and onward to the contemporary period, with Rousseau and other Enlightenment thinkers, there has been a consistent devaluing of the body, which has filtered down to teachers and scholars. That devaluing leads to a dismissive attitude about the importance of thinking philosophically about the body. Due to lingering dualistic trends in culture and religion, mind is often privileged over matter, reason over emotion, and the soul over the body. What is often meant by the "body," according to such a dualistic perspective, is the flesh that holds one back in life. This view has understood women's bodies as distractions to men and historically has seen brown and black bodies as inhuman, allowing them to be

> Aren't war and poverty more important issues for Christians to deal with than fashion and popular culture?

commodified and sold throughout modern times. Devaluing the body and disregarding issues related to embodiment foster a social context that understands the body as a problem, an entity that needs to be controlled and scaled. This mentality seeps into all aspects of our embodied being, and at times we feel ashamed of our shopping, eating, sexual desires, and even our dress practices. When the issue is framed in this light, it probably is not surprising at all that a bodily practice like adorning ourselves would be understood as not intellectual enough to discuss at length.

Throughout the latter half of the twentieth century, however, feminists and other liberation theorists worked diligently to prioritize thinking about the body in critical terms. They began to conceptualize the body as a powerful vehicle of communication and embodied activities as places where social power is negotiated. They began to articulate how dualistic mentalities, which subjugate the body to the mind and some bodies to other bodies, result in exploitative and oppressive social structures—including ones that subjugate women to men, blacks to whites, and animals to humans. In light of these theoretical developments, we are obliged to ask whether in fact the body is a problem. If what we mean by "problem" is something to be avoided, overcome, discarded, or even normalized, then I do not think the body is a problem. However, if we embrace the sense of the body as a social and historical text that requires sustained attention and reflection so that individuals and groups can build life-giving relationships with God and others, then, yes, certainly the body and all processes associated with it represent theological and philosophical problems worthy of engagement.

The body problem does not end there. Now, more than ever—with the proliferation of electronic communication technology, including the Internet, social media, and texting—new challenges arise in understanding the meanings and values associated with the body and embodied experience. Some have argued that virtual life and gaming have led to a disembodied reality in which our bodies seem insignificant and even disappear. Obviously, our bodies don't really vanish. We still have to take breaks from e-mailing and texting to eat and sleep, among other embodied activities. Nevertheless, it is fascinating to think about how we can hide our bodies behind avatars and mute our true feelings with carefully scripted e-mails and texts. In his book *Hiding*, Mark C. Taylor theorizes two somewhat opposing effects related to the phenomenon of the disappearing body: "For some people, the growing detachment from the body holds the promise of realizing the ancient dream of immortality; for others, the apparent loss of the body and eclipse of materiality are further symptoms of alienation."[1] In an effort to bring back their bodies into existence and rewrite their stories, many people, according to Taylor, are turning to body art: "Tattooing represents the effort to mark the body at the very moment it is disappearing."[2] Attentiveness to such embodied rituals and the stories they tell is an important component of developing a spirituality of dress. With each shirt, surgery, diet, piercing, and tattoo or even decision to go naked, we reveal our stories. We communicate values, ethics, and identity, along with hopes, dreams, and anxieties—all dimensions of existence that are most worthy of study and discussion.

One final red flag I want to acknowledge when analyzing the philosophical and religious meaning behind our clothing comes from an almost contradictory position: that only the elite have time to think about these body issues. Interestingly, when juxtaposed with one another, these challenges seem to contradict one another. The first argues that a spirituality of clothing is not academic

> From Plato to Paul, from Augustine to Aquinas, and onward to the contemporary period, with Rousseau and other Enlightenment thinkers, there has been a consistent devaluing of the body.

enough, while the second claims that only academics have time for such queries. It is not that the body is elite, but rather that the study of it and its related social practices is an activity available only to privileged individuals. That is an important issue indeed, since if and when we do have one of these mirror moments, few of us of have the luxury of time to seriously consider and reflect on what is happening, never mind ask the big questions about freedom. We are so pressured to make breakfast for our children, check our e-mail, pay overdue bills, and get to work on time that the big questions fade, and we become lulled into thinking that what we wear and why we wear it is no more than a result of our personal tastes and economic resources. Yet this book rests on the premise that while our style and finances certainly influence our clothing, when we actually do slow down and reflect on what we wear and why we wear it, we may be surprised by the answers. How we adorn ourselves reveals our feelings and attitudes, particularly our anxieties, about our relationships with ourselves, others, God, and all the messy borders in between. While many of us don't have time to explore our mirror moments, the effort might improve our quality of life if we made time for it.

What's in a Name?

I use three terms—*clothing, dress*, and *adornment*—interchangeably throughout this book, since they all refer in one way or another to the act of putting on or taking off garments and other body modifications as a way to perform one's identity. The term *clothing* appears frequently in the Bible and along with the term *dress* is the most succinct way of describing what many of us do daily—put on clothes and accessories in order to participate in the social world. Beyond biblical references, the Christian imagination is full of allusions to clothing. Many Christians are familiar with stories about John the Baptist's camel hair clothing and Francis of Assisi's burlap robe. Closer to home, many female students, particularly the ones raised as Catholics, are all too ready to discuss their First Communions, specifically how they felt about wearing a white dress and veil at the tender age of seven. In each of these contexts, clothing symbolizes a different aspect of the Christian story. John's clothing communicates his prophetic qualities, while Francis's robe symbolizes the Franciscan commitment to poverty and a life of self-denial. My students' Communion dresses express a sense of purity and newness.

Another way to describe how clothing tells a story is to use the language of adornment. The connotation of the term *adornment* pushes the discussion to include the varied body modification regimens we use as part of our dress on a daily basis. These include but are not limited to the articles of clothing we put on and how we arrange them, hair care and style, cosmetics, accessories, dieting, weight training, plastic surgery, hygiene products, perfumes, dental care, nail and skin care, jewelry, piercing, tattooing, and circumcision. The borders between our bodies and our dress are becoming increasingly murky, especially with the rise of tattooing and piercing in global capitalist cultures, to the extent that some theorists have referred to this enmeshment between body and dress as movement toward cyborg being. Advances in communication technology further what is meant by clothing. Mobile phones, BlackBerry devices, iPods, and Bluetooth devices are all part of one's dress or adornment. We decorate our bodies in ways our grandparents and parents might never have imagined. Some "bedazzle" their phones with crystals and other accessories. Our clothing is made to suit our technology. For example, now there are shirts and sleeves available to accommodate one's iPad and smartphone.

In his famous text, *The Psychology of Clothes*, J. C. Flugel claims that when we adorn or decorate ourselves, we signal who we are and what our values are, communicating publicly our most personal stories and our deepest anxieties, making dress an "extension of our bodily self."[3] At the same time, when we tell someone we like his or her outfit, we are usually commenting on the person's whole look, extending to how that look performs the person's identity—the way tattoos complement clothing, the way hair complements makeup. Whether we are preschoolers playing in our mothers' closets, tweens celebrating Halloween, or adults getting ready for work, we all in a way are playing dress-up. We consciously and unconsciously employ our clothing, dress, and adornment practices to reveal our identities and stories to the world.

Whatever term makes us comfortable—clothing, dress, or adornment—it is arguable that clothing does not end with what we put on, shape, or mold; it also includes what we take off or leave bare. In effect, when we get naked, we are adorning ourselves. This is an important idea to think about at the very least, because it calls into question whether there is any natural or normal mode of dress. We like to think of being naked as simply being without clothes. Sometimes we think of nakedness as symbolic of innocence, a blank script even. This leads to conflating naked with natural. There is a common sense logic to this: we are born naked, so nakedness seems natural. What if, however, we are tattooed, pierced, or circumcised—are we still naked or natural? Is a shaved naked body natural? How has the proliferation of plastic surgery changed the face of what is natural and what it means to be naked? When the missionaries encountered the indigenous peoples, did they think the natives were natural in their nakedness?

Following the lead of so much of the feminist theory that has shaped and continues to influence our understanding of identity, in this book I argue that bodies are always mediating meaning, in that we are never naked if what we mean by naked is "without meaning." Even through the barest of images, our bodies perform who we are to the world, and that meaning is negotiated between subject and other. By extension, all aspects of our identity, including our gender, race, class, and ethnicity, are wittingly or unwittingly performed. Every outfit we wear carries meaning and reflects our story, even when our dress is that of nakedness. Perhaps nakedness is a type of clothing and form of dress—it is a performance, a story, a communiqué. This notion of nakedness as an adornment practice is especially important in this book, since I begin to imagine the incarnation as a kenotic event and model for all, a moment in which God gets naked in solidarity with human beings. Through the incarnation, God dresses in vulnerability. This reading has the potential to change how Christians think and feel about their finitude, creating the possibility for transforming vulnerability from being a bad word into a good one—namely, an invitation to develop more genuine relationships of interdependence within their lives.

> What if, however, we are tattooed, pierced, or circumcised—are we still naked or natural? Is a shaved naked body natural? How has the proliferation of plastic surgery changed the face of what is natural and what it means to be naked?

When we imagine a spirituality of dress, then, our thoughts travel at least three trajectories. The first is understanding that what we wear, why we wear it, and all the anxieties around those processes have meaning in culture. The second involves questioning the value of the patterns of dress we are enmeshed in, assessing which are life-giving and which lead to brokenness. And a third trajectory reenvisions the incarnation as a form of dress that has the potential to norm all others for believers. This last claim is not intended to be exclusionary to non-Christians. It rather represents one key for thinking about vulnerability as a sacred sign of God's hospitality for and solidarity with creatures.

Overview of the Book

I have divided this book into three chapters, which loosely follow those three trajectories. Chapter 1 focuses on the anxiety related to our adornment practices. Humans are faced with a paradox of having been created in the image of God and being finite, having glorious promise and being constrained by their mortality. The stress of living this paradox can be a good thing, particularly when we draw on the resulting anxiety to stretch ourselves emotionally, physically, and spiritually. Reflecting on the creation narratives in Genesis 1 and 2, I elaborate on how each of us in our everyday practice of dress has the option of transforming stress about human existence into a catalyst for creating life-giving relationships with God and others. Then, referring to Genesis 3 and the fall of Adam and Eve, I focus on the downside of our anxiety. I illustrate how vulnerability and mortality are dimensions of human existence that have become distorted into something negative and perverse—shameful signs of our powerlessness. When vulnerability is perceived this way, we dress to shield ourselves from the emotional, psychological, and spiritual stress caused by our own or another's negative judgments about our human frailties.

When directing our anxiety into something positive, we would like to think we have unencumbered freedom and choice about what to wear and why we wear it. We will see, however, that freedom is curtailed by external stress-ors, including the fashion industry, global consumerist culture, and even our families. I argue that for the good effects of our anxiety to take hold, we need to be cognizant of the impact of these stressors on our freedom. Also, I claim that for a spirituality of dress to emerge, we must reenvision freedom in light of our vulnerabilities. When we embrace our limits, even through something as ordi-nary and mundane as our dress, a more life-giving sense of freedom emerges, one in which we are thoughtful about and responsible for our interconnections with others locally and globally.

In chapter 2, I focus more specifically on how failure to engage with issues related to our dress opens up our-selves and others to brokenness. Focusing on popular ideas about dress as a way to achieve happiness, I prompt readers to question the messages we hand down to our loved ones. By passing on hand-me-downs, such as, "If you look good, you feel good," or the commonsense notion that retail therapy and dressing up are cathartic, I argue that we actively participate in the brokenness of the world. We pass on sin, not necessarily through our dress, but rather through our lack of attention to or, perhaps worse, our blindness to the negative implications of these hand-me-downs. Christian discipleship depends on struggling against these patterns of blindness, or what an important Roman Catholic theologian named Bernard Lonergan called *scotomas*, in an effort to recover from the decline associated with our anxiety about mortality.[4]

Next, shifting from the personal to the political, I ask what, if anything, is sinful about our contemporary prac-tices of adornment in a global world. Taking on the issue of where our clothes come from, I analyze how sin and grace manifest uniquely in everyone's adornment auto-biography. As in the previous section, I invite readers to reflect on their own dress experience—this time with an eye toward global justice. The results of this self-story time will vary. For example, tracing one's clothing to a company that employs child labor stimulates a profoundly different reaction than tracing one's dress to a company in which the workers make a living wage. Telling one's own story related to what one wears and why one wears it is an important step toward embracing vulnerability locally and globally.

In the third chapter, I rethink trajectories in scripture and tradition that foster engagement with serious questions about our how our daily regimens of dress influence Christian discipleship. In particular, I explore moments in our dress that call us to be hospitable to and in solidarity with others in need. Scriptural passages on exodus and exile, biblical and popular narratives about Jesus' parents (Mary and Joseph), and snapshots of Jesus' other-oriented activity in the Gospels all reveal a sense that human beings are not just born vulnerable but called to embrace their neediness as a way to create community. Most intensely, however, I highlight Christian claims about the incarnation as a form of dress. For believers, when God becomes human in the person of Jesus Christ, he exposes himself, gets naked, and takes on human vulnerability. In the last pages of the book, I hope to convince readers that Christians are called to bear witness to the incarnation by being thoughtful about and committed to the importance of vulnerability in their adornment practices. I hope to demonstrate that "getting naked" with Jesus, or embracing our vulnerability, is our only hope at creating life-giving relationships with God and others in the global world. Stephanie Paulsell's work *Honoring the Body: Meditations on a Christian Practice* comes to mind here, as she asserts that being human in a way that engenders life-giving relationships in local and global contexts depends on embracing our "sacred vulnerability," our limits, all the while being oriented toward God.[5]

Moving from theory to practice, I then ask how Christians might embrace vulnerability concretely in their everyday lives, to the point of making vulnerability fashionable. People need to buy into the importance of embracing their sacred vulnerability in order to transform the sinful patterns of consumption, debt, and exploitation that characterize our current adornment practices worldwide. Some individuals and groups are already doing this. One example is TOMS Shoes. For each pair of shoes it sells, TOMS donates a pair of shoes to a needy child. And SweatFree Communities is an organization that supports workers in sweatshops worldwide in an effort to transform the global economy and enact just practices. Making vulnerability fashionable opens us up to these possibilities and more.

1

vulnerability and the human condition

"Therefore I tell you, do not worry about your life, what you will eat or what you will drink, or about your body, what you will wear. Is not life more than food, and the body more important than clothing?"

Matthew 6:25

Human beings have a limited tolerance for feeling vulnerable. Sure, when babies are born, we honor their fragile nature and embrace it as part of the miracle of life. We swathe them with our warmest blankets and softest clothes and bathe their delicate bodies with soothing cleansers and lotions. We cherish the helplessness of infants, accepting their limits without question, at times being contented by their dependence on us. In most cases, we are comfortable with their messiness and unpredictability, changing their diapers at inconvenient times and feeding them at all hours of the day. We expect them neither to have control over their embodied selves nor to be perfect.

However, as the years pass, our expectations and comfort level regarding their vulnerability slowly change. Children's parents, along with their physicians, teachers, and caregivers, track and foster the children's growth out of this original state of dependence. We anticipate development from this fragile and vulnerable condition toward reaching the appropriate physical and social milestones. We have patience throughout the process. As babies begin to walk, we don't ridicule them when they fall. Instead, we keep encouraging them toward their goal. When children begin to dress themselves, we forgive and even embrace their mismatched socks and bunched-up pants because we know they are learning and this state of disarray is temporary.

Without fail, as children grow up, our acceptance of their limits wanes, and we find that the world is far less forgiving of their frailties. Messy bodies are understood to be in need of fixing, so much so that as soon as children step onto the playground, they are strongly encouraged, if not bullied, into acting and—more important for this conversation—into *looking* a certain way. A clumsy gait is no longer cute, but rather a possible first sign of a developmental delay. Runny noses could symbolize poor hygiene, and last year's fashions often signify a lower social and economic status. Neediness is read as a sign of weakness. Children are faced head-on with implicit social rules about their body and embodied practices to which they must conform. Nonconformity risks at the very least scorn, and at the very worst being treated as less than human. All of us experience an unsaid but deeply felt correlation between the norms of dress and the norms of humanity.

Perhaps the pressure on children today is not this bleak, and I am being too sensitive to growing pains. Yet few make it through childhood without experiencing some of these stressors, creating anxiety that transcends their childhood and follows them into adulthood. Clearly, beyond playground politics, the college students I encounter report that when they go on their first job interviews, they must prepare to meet certain expectations about dress and clothing taboos as well. For instance, they tell me that while most of their peers have tattoos and piercings, having too many is unfavorable in professional contexts. So if they really want the work, they need to cover up the tattoos with long sleeves and remove the nose rings.

What I am hoping to illustrate here is that at every stage of our life, what we wear and why we wear it largely result from a negotiation of anxiety about what is expected, what is the norm, and what is considered human. Nonconformance to social expectations is at times read as a sign of weakness, of not being properly socialized, and even a scar on our humanity. The bottom line is that showing weakness and vulnerability either on the playground or in the boardroom is unappealing to others and often a liability. Yet even though we learn from early childhood on that our clothing has the potential to hide our human frailties and neediness, and we struggle to adhere to what is considered "normal" rather than "deviant," many of us barely pass the test, and our humanity is challenged. The impossible ideal of perfection, which seems to be the new look for humanity, is always just beyond our reach.

The pressure to be perfect and have total control over one's body at all times is ubiquitous. If school and work don't convince us that to be human is to keep our bodies in check, the media are quite effective in spreading the news. Every time we turn on our television or surf the Internet, this or that advertisement practically brainwashes us into believing the idea that if we adorn ourselves appropriately and perfectly, we can escape teasing and succeed in life. Some scholars, particularly those in the field of disability studies, refer to the cultural notion that we can and ought to control our bodies in order to be successful and happy as the "myth of control."[1] *Success* is one of the slippery terms and in this context usually means being in control of life, not being dependent on others, and practically being perfect. Conversely, feeling mentally, physically, or spiritually out of control, being dependent and interconnected with others in complicated relationships, not fitting into the norm, and being less than perfect are framed as problems that need to be overcome. A question to ponder is whether vulnerability is always part of the human condition. If the answer is yes, then why do we hide from it, and why does it make us so anxious? In other words, *why do we worry?* We may not need diapers, but someday we might. We may not need bibs, but when we are tired and as we age, drooling can and does happen. Once we mature, we may be able to live on our own, but we always need companions to enrich our life journey. When framed this way, neediness is part of creaturely existence.

Vulnerability as a Fact of Life

Jean Vanier, a Canadian Catholic thinker and humanitarian, has devoted his life to demonstrating that vulnerability, far from being aberrant and abject, is a universal and transcultural norm in all creatures. For Vanier, we do not grow out of vulnerability; on the contrary, we grow into it. Our embrace of being limited, vulnerable, and mortal is the catalyst for our true freedom. Vanier is founder of L'Arche, a global network of residential communities where traditionally "abled" and "disabled" people live in Christian fellowship, appreciating the other's humanity and gifts. This experience allows him to see the grace of vulnerability in all relationships, even as an invitation to communion with God and others. In his work *Becoming Human*, Vanier describes how each one of us is called to open up to our vulnerability, to imagine our neediness as way to connect with others and God, as an invitation for deep, sacramental relationships.[2] He argues further that exposing ourselves to this physical, emotional, and spiritual nakedness is what makes us human. Reading Vanier, one intuits that we are chosen as creatures to enact our freedom in ways that expose our neediness to others. Our neediness then is not only a fact of life, but also a gift that orients us and our freedom toward others.

> In consumer culture, we have come to believe, as the English philosopher Herbert Spencer once noted, that our dress can provide us with a "peace" that religion fails to offer us.

This is a vastly different sense of freedom from the one in which many of us have been raised—an individualistic and privatized notion of freedom in which the totality of our choices are geared toward personal advancement regardless of the cost to those around us. To be free in this commonsense way requires that we hide and suppress all feelings of vulnerability, as they have become conflated with powerlessness. At least for the past century, in the industrialized, capitalized superpower nations, to be human means to be powerful, to make it on one's own, and not to need anyone for help. It is interesting that from somewhat of a skewed Christian perspective, many of us have been socialized into thinking and feeling that being limited is a fault that needs to be rectified, even a *sin* that requires purgation and payment. We have lost sight of the reality that being creaturely is correlative to being imperfect. As a result, we have a blind spot that fools us into thinking we can overcome our weaknesses.

When we begin to really think about our dress habits, we may come to see that clothing allows us to cover up our so-called sins and mask all our uncomfortable feelings about being creatures with limits. Not all dress is used for this purpose, since sometimes we use dress to cover up from the dangerous elements of our environment, such as the seasonal climates of heat and cold. Without gloves in a snowstorm, we risk the pain of frostbite. Without sunscreen to block the damaging ultraviolet rays in the summer, we risk the suffering associated with sunburns or, even worse, skin cancer. These are practical instances in which clothing allows us to survive. Still, much of the time, our adornment practices are far from pragmatic and rather more a way of conforming to social pressures and satiating desires to be accepted as "normal." We don't wear just any hat or boots; instead, we dress to meet social expectations and match up with norms of style, class, gender, religion, and so on. We dress to look good, which makes us feel less anxious about our social standing. Our clothing wields cultural capital in that it protects us from negative judgments by our peers. In consumer culture, we have come to believe, as the English philosopher Herbert Spencer once noted, that our dress can provide us with a "peace" that religion fails to offer us.[3] Unfortunately, more often than not, this "peace," or high even, is short-lived. If we are unable to adorn ourselves or our loved ones with the "right stuff," whatever that is, we experience a terrible low, an unsettling anxiety, throwing us into a cycle of decline. In this way, dress has become an accomplice to humanity's denial of limits, fostering distorted conceptions of human existence and resulting in destructive relationships.

For Vanier, and imaginably many Christians who are trying to live as Jesus did, this interpretation of what it means to be human is dangerous. It is disturbing to conceptualize human limits and vulnerability as something to be avoided, especially when Christians are called both to imitate a messiah who seeks out the vulnerable in society and who embraces exposure on the cross, and to worship a God who through the incarnation becomes human in the fullest sense, including that of having limits and being vulnerable. Vanier hopes to show that this perverse reading of vulnerability and the resulting self-centered notion of freedom fail to reflect the spirit of the Christian tradition and damage our capacity for well-being. While such notions of freedom that are related to being independent and being in control may appear to support our flourishing, the effect is short-lived and superficial, leaving us with what he calls a "false" sense of self, whereby our freedom closes us in on ourselves. To "become human," we have to risk living without this pretense of being free for ourselves only and accept the liminality of relationships with all types of individuals and communities. For Vanier and others like him, being human is a process that takes work, including vigilance about how we understand our sense of self and use our freedom in relation to others, and here we would be right to include all others—human beings, animals, plants, and so on.

Thinking about vulnerability as a fact of life and a gift from God sets the stage for examining how our dress practices reflect our understanding of freedom and their impact on our quality of life. One way to understand clothing is as a fluid, porous border between ourselves and others, in which what we wear and why we wear it have as much effect on others as on ourselves. When framed this way, our dress bonds us to all others, creatures and the creator alike, in an intimate and profound way. In getting dressed, we have the choice of acknowledging this border not only for the good of ourselves but for all creatures. Do we dress in a way that is hospitable and in solidarity with others, or in a way that cuts off relationships with them? These are the types of issues and questions that Vanier's work stimulates. Exposing our vulnerability in genuine, embodied relationships can be beautiful, and by revealing our needs for another's love, touch, and protection, we open ourselves to the depths of the human heart.

Vulnerability and the Real World. Some of the college students I encounter hope to get a job that pays enough for them to live in the city, while others are on their way to graduate school or service internships. Whatever their story and aspirations, most really appreciate Vanier's insights about healthy relationships and commitment to the marginalized and, as previously mentioned, Paulsell's attentiveness to body as a site of sacred vulnerability. Yet they are quick to interject that vulnerability and neediness are not readily accepted in Western consumerist culture. On more than one occasion, students have pressed me on this simple question: *What's so great about vulnerability?* Sometimes they put it this way: *If we are all trying so hard to avoid being vulnerable, why would we work so hard to embrace it?* One student wanted the bottom line on accepting vulnerability by asking, "What's the incentive?"

These are the tough and important questions—the "so what?" factor, as I like to put it. I want to respond in a way that confirms the rigor and genuineness of such critical analysis, not with a stilted catechetical response like "Christians believe God made humans that way," or "The incarnation sacralizes that lived reality." Even though these points are sound, such a quick response is insensitive to students' concerns, especially as some do not consider themselves particularly religious. Although their skepticism does not come out of the blue, I find myself fumbling around as if this were the first time I had been confronted with these questions. I manage to give an abbreviated yet affirming response, but my students want and deserve more. We all feel a ton of pressure to demonstrate that we have our lives under control and that we do not need much of anything from anyone. I experience those pressures and the negative stress associated with the students. So before I get to the theological responses, I empathize with them. I know firsthand that exposing one's feelings about being less than perfect and in control—needing others—can be terrifying. What if the thing or person we need is unavailable or just plain uninterested in being in a relationship? I, too, at times wonder about what is so good about being limited, about being confined to the laws of time and space, about being mortal, and about fundamentally being unable to survive without others, particularly in a culture that prides itself on the values of independence, individualism, and autonomy. These concerns catapult us to the shadow side of vulnerability, where neediness becomes a dirty word.

Dress, like many of the other embodied practices we engage in every day, negotiates these two sides of creaturely existence—the vulnerability that invites relationship and the vulnerability that repels it. While all might benefit from embracing vulnerability as a fact of life,

Christians in particular—since they believe human frailty to be sacramentalized in the incarnation, in God becoming human—are obligated to deal with this tension, to imagine vulnerability as a way of connecting to others, and to reject any notion that vulnerability is a defect or sin. Beginning here may provide a well-deserved response to the "so what?" factor that is less sickeningly sweet and ultimately more honest. Moreover, as a side note, the desire to overcome our vulnerability is futile, since we can never get beyond our finitude, our here-and-nowness, our mortality. When we fail to recognize the futility of this desire, we risk squandering important opportunities to develop deeper and more life-giving relationships with others.

So back to my student's million-dollar question: *What's the incentive?* The answer for me is *the good life*—a life in which we are genuinely free, in a way analogous to what Vanier envisions, whereby freedom is activated by exposing our humanity to the other. Fear constricts our choices, and when we relinquish and/or transform our anxieties about our humanity from fear to hope, we are opened to new horizons and new heights.

Anxiety and the Human Condition. Dealing with human apprehension about being mortal, and thus about having limits, is not new. Throughout history, theologians, philosophers, and of course clinicians in the fields of psychology and psychiatry have been concerned about the effects of this anxiety on human existence. One of the world's great religions, Buddhism, teaches us that desire brings suffering, and we need to overcome that desire to reach enlightenment. Christians also have conceptual frames for explaining the damaging effects of desire. In *The Nature and Destiny of Man*, Reinhold Niebuhr, a prominent American Protestant theologian of the twentieth century, claims that a fundamental challenge to human existence is the anxiety caused by our desire to be perfect and godlike, even with the knowledge that creaturely existence is characterized by limits and, of course, mortality.[4] This anxiety is not necessarily sinful, according to Niebuhr, yet if it is not acknowledged and worked through, it has the potential to cause pain and suffering and lead to sin and brokenness.

When read this way, anxiety presents an invitation to find out what drives us and whether that is healthy and life-giving. In not paying attention to moments of anxiety over feeling vulnerable, and even denying that anxiety with a pretense of being superhuman or above it all, we may find ourselves in negative patterns of self-loathing. In the context of the daily practice of clothing, we may be repeatedly disappointed in what we look like, perhaps developing eating disorders and body dysmorphic disorders, which harm girls and boys, women and men. This is only part of the problem. We also could end up passing on these patterns of self-loathing and fear of being vulnerable to our loved ones, and perhaps integrating them into our market economies, leading to damaged relationships within local and global arenas. As we work toward constructing a spirituality of dress, I hope we can begin to imagine moments of feeling anxious as requests to learn more about our relationships with others in the world. As such, that anxiety is not always a bad thing.

This may need further explanation, as many of us go to great measures to avoid anxiety in our everyday lives. We value mental and physical exercises, such as prayer and yoga, that reduce the harmful effects of stress. We pay a lot of money and sometimes endure burdensome side effects for pharmaceuticals to alleviate some of the more extreme cases of anxiety, in which people are unable to participate in ordinary daily activities. Such exercise and medications are great gifts, particularly in the success stories where lower stress levels have improved people's quality of life. At the same time, some instances of anxiety can be helpful, particularly moments of stress that move us to understand more clearly our needs and the needs of others. Feeling anxious creates the possibility for pausing in our everyday activities, reflecting on why we are doing what we are doing, and even transforming patterns that threaten our well-being and that of others. Anxiety can be a catalyst for imagining a healthier living environment and for sustaining the best of Christian community. Regardless of one's level of piety, it is beneficial to think about the everyday practices of clothing, to examine if and how our adornment practices serve to cover up our anxieties about the neediness of being a creature, as well as to consider the possibilities of retrieving vulnerability as a virtue rather than a vice.

What to Wear?

Whether we have been preparing for an exciting event such as a wedding or a somber occasion such as a loved one's funeral, we all have had to deal with this one seemingly innocuous question: *What am I going to wear?* For some, answering the question is exciting, producing what we might call an adrenaline high. Planning an outfit allows us to show off our creativity, to tell the world who we really are, and to attract friends and lovers—in other words, to relate and connect to people and the world through our clothing. At other times (sometimes at the same times), the simple question of what to wear is enough to stress anyone out. Limited resources may hinder our ability to purchase the right clothes or any at all. We may not fit into the fashionable styles, for not everyone can wear "skinny" jeans. We may even be forbidden from wearing what we want or what makes us feel comfortable. All these obstacles can cause us to feel anxious and overwhelmed.

Do Not Worry? As already alluded to in the beginning of the chapter, the gospels of Matthew and Luke portray Jesus as warning his followers against worrying about what to wear and what to eat, urging them instead to "strive first for the kingdom of God and his righteousness, and all these things will be given to [them] as well" (Matthew 6:33). Nevertheless, living in consumerist culture, one is hard-pressed not to worry. In fact, getting dressed has the opposite effect, stressing us out to the point at which we are practically consumed and worn away by the thought of it.

In these instances, a better reading of the gospel may be to *pay attention* to what we are worrying about, rather than *not to worry*. For in being attentive and acknowledging the worry, we take a step toward overcoming and transforming that worry if it is death-dealing. Embracing the stress of what to wear creates a moment to examine how vulnerability and freedom unfold in the human condition and how dress is a potential symbol of a commitment to life-giving relationships with God and others. In the words

> In the words of Stephanie Paulsell, feeling stressed out could motivate Christians to imagine that "the daily clothing of our bodies illuminate[s] our invisible baptismal garb."

of Paulsell, feeling stressed out could motivate Christians to imagine that "the daily clothing of our bodies illuminate[s] our invisible baptismal garb."[5] For Christians, baptism commences a lifetime of imagining dress as a way of being human that respects God and others, whereby we are called to embrace vulnerability within ourselves and with others as a way of connecting with them. Facing our anxiety about what to wear may provide moments to renew our baptismal promises and reflect further on how we can dress in a way that orients us for life-giving relationships with others.

What's so great about vulnerability?

Struggling with the issue of what to wear is not just a Christian concern; many individuals and groups already pay attention to how their clothing affects others. Some are vigilant about where they shop and how the workers who produce and sell the apparel are treated. They are concerned about whether the workers are compensated with a living wage and whether children are being exploited at any point of the process. Others are vigilant about knowing who or what is used in testing out cosmetic products and surgical procedures. Still others, most obviously feminists, are troubled by the way social norms force individuals into rigid gender categories, making one choose between a living a girl's story or a boy's story through their dress. From a myriad of angles, intellectuals and ordinary folk pose important questions about the stories we tell about what we wear and why we wear it, as well as about the effects of those stories on the others around us, rendering storytelling an important dimension of a spirituality of dress.

Clothing as Story. Ever since I was a little girl, I can remember how much anticipation and preparation went into dressing for a party. Whether it was a new dress for Easter, my First Communion dress, or as I got older, what I would wear for a night out on the town, the big question then and now is what to wear. Planning the right dress is a way to tell my story, to reveal who I am and who I aspire to be. Each one us has stories, and in acknowledging our stories about what we wear and why we wear it, and reflecting on them and sharing them, we may find that others have similar anxieties and worries, and perhaps even find hope and grace in them.

In a poignant essay, "Jewish Genes, Jewish Jeans: A Fashionable Body," Karin Anijar recollects her mother's funeral in Miami, expressing how so much of her Jewish identity has been negotiated through dress.[6] Since the casket is late to arrive for the funeral service, Anijar has to explain the delay to the mourners. She apologizes to the crowd and half-jokes when she announces, "Mother is late. It seems there was a sale at Neiman-Marcus (an up-scale department store)."[7] As Anijar weaves clothing practices with autobiography, we catch a glimpse into how shopping and having a certain type of look facilitated the assimilation of Jewish immigrants and their families into American culture. A hilarious and heartwarming essay, yet more than that, Anijar's work is challenging in that it invites readers to think about how our adornment practices tell our stories, locating us into certain identities, signifying all sorts of codes about gender, race, nationality, citizenship, and religion. What does a specific pair of shoes symbolize about our ethnicity, or how does a certain cosmetic procedure reveal our story about who we are and what our struggles have been? Christians might learn from Anijar's work that storytelling is an important component of spirituality. Conceptualizing our clothing in terms of symbol and story—as autobiography—challenges us to narrate who we are publicly, to think about the choices we make in our adornment practices, and to embrace all the anxieties we face about finitude.

It is worth bearing in mind that, at least on the intuitive level, there is a slight difference between symbol and story. A particular item of clothing might have symbolic meaning in that it points to a particular referent. Sometimes symbols are easy to read; for instance, when someone is wearing a certain sports jersey, it usually means the person is a fan of that particular team. However, if someone is wearing a cross pendant on a necklace, the symbolic referent may be more ambiguous. It could refer to the individual's belonging to the Christian religion, or perhaps it is merely a fashion statement. For a while, celebrities were wearing crosses all the time, seemingly not for religious reasons, but rather just because they were in style. This is where reading symbol necessitates story in that knowing the individual's story aids our understanding of the connection between a specific item of clothing or dress practice and the identity of the individual in question. That knowledge comes only from mutually sharing one's thoughts and feelings about what we wear and why we wear it. Similarly, wearing a pink ribbon symbolizes support of breast cancer awareness and research, but to really know the dresser's story, we have to ask questions about his or her life, and the person has to share. Is the person closely related to someone who has had breast cancer? What is the person's story?

Some dress stories are more complicated than others, especially when told interculturally. Explaining the culture of Afghan women in the United States and the practice of veiling, also known as *hijab*, M. Catherine Daly argues that, to outsiders (meaning those unaware of the Afghan ethnicity), all veils look alike.[8] For insiders, in contrast, each particular veil marks differences in country, class, and so on, dependent on the material, colors, and other features. In this example, reading another's story is far from obvious. In situations like these, instead of assuming one knows what this or that symbolizes, it might bode well to ask the person about his or her apparel directly and honestly. This is not necessarily being intrusive, but trying to be educated and even "connect" with another person on an interpersonal level. In such an exchange, both parties really need to listen to the other person's story about dress, rather than making all sorts of assumptions.

Even after having read this essay on *hijab* in my Religion and the Body course, students sometimes still have difficulty embracing the full story of Muslim dress and unwittingly fall back into stereotypes about Islam and the "oppression" of Muslim women. Many students scoff at the words of the Muslim women who say they feel freer when veiled. Students explicitly or implicitly assert that these women are deluding themselves and must be victims of some sort of false consciousness. Every so often, when one brave student in the class turns to the others and asks how their own cultural dress practices might be seen as oppressive, the conversation becomes even more intense and complicated. Questions such as these arise: Are U.S. secularized women really free when they are supposed to wear stiletto heels and midriff shirts as a sign of their femininity? Aren't we all, regardless of specific culture and custom, constrained by norms of dress? What often ensues in class discussion is the argument that not all norms are bad; rather, the refusal to allow for any sort of deviance from the norm is potentially harmful and damaging. Moreover, students begin to argue that when individuals and groups name people as deviant without paying attention to the meanings and values of the specific culture to which they belong, this, too, has the potential to become damaging and even lead to violence. A good example of this occurred when Christian missionaries labeled non-Christians as heathens in need of saving, largely due to their difference in dress and appearance. This dangerous phenomenon of "otherizing" continues into the present day against any who deviate from Western norms.

Most of us don't otherize people because we are mean; we don't exclude and bully them because we have deep pathological problems. Many of us resort to such tactics because we are so afraid of not being accepted, of not being in control, and, even worse, of others finding out that we are less than perfect. We like to know who the boy is and who the girl is, so we know how to behave toward them. We like to know what is considered civilized and what is considered uncivilized, so we know how to act. Ambiguity in any of these scenarios has the potential to reveal our vulnerability and our anxiety about it. Taylor argues that the contemporary rage of tattooing is a way of signifying all the ambivalence we feel and ambiguity that exists in the world between what is savage and civilized, what is normal and abnormal.[9] From this perspective, adorning our body is a way to navigate the stressful complex web of creaturely existence.

As one might imagine, engaging in these sorts of conversations about the messiness of embodied existence in life and in the classroom leads to touchy moments when we find ourselves walking on eggshells to avoid offending others or coming off as self-righteous. With caution we proceed. We know someone can get hurt by our words, so we tread lightly. We begin to realize that freedom in dress is a complicated concept, especially when we begin to think about how norms of dress organize our worldview, our sense of right and wrong and of good and evil. Norms of dress define what it means to be human and what it means to be something or someone else. In those touchy moments when we feel uneasy about either our dress or that of another, we are invited to dig deep and question how dress fosters either grace or brokenness. This is really difficult work, as it asks us to think about issues we never really have time for and because it is personal and even emotionally painful. Telling our stories and admitting to these touchy moments is a risk-filled process. Delving into our adornment practices will in all likelihood reveal discrepancies, contradictions, and anxieties about what is socially acceptable, what a normal body looks like, and even more basically, what is normal as opposed to deviant. While a course on Religion and the Body is a more than apropos venue for such discussions, Christians in all contexts would benefit from sharing their dress stories—the ones that bring good stress, the ones that bring bad stress, and the ones that bring both—as they work to create a more life-giving community with God and others.

Good Stress

Thinking back to all those events in my life that were dotted with dresses and crossed with new hairstyles, I honestly can say that at times (not all the time), the question of what to wear resulted in stress that was positive, motivating, and inspiring. Moreover, each of my outfits represented personal stories of hope—for good times, life-giving friendships, and a happy future. Even though as a child I never thought of clothing this way, as an adult—as a woman, a mother, and a teacher—I have come to realize that there is a positive energy in planning what to wear. Clothing encourages us to be creative and imaginative and to open up to others in all our human vulnerability and frailty.

Furthermore, dress is not merely the life story of an individual. Communities experience and exhibit hope through their dress as well. In some African American communities, wearing one's best to Sunday services, complete with elaborate hairdos and costly clothing, is an important part of celebrating the congregants' embodied selves—bodies that historically have been raped, lynched, mutilated, and murdered. Gwendolyn S. O'Neal explains that all the anxiety and stressors related to their Sunday dress actually moves African Americans toward the good in that it hopes for a freedom previously unattainable.[10] When framed this way, adornment is an exercise in preparing ourselves for salvation, both here on earth and in the world to come, for the here and now and the hereafter.

While the preceding examples certainly capture some of the good feelings and hopeful thoughts related to clothing, there is a danger in using the phrase *good stress* in regard to our dress practices. That danger comes from a tendency to conflate good stress with happy times. As I understand it here, good stress does not emerge only in pleasant occasions, but rather in any dress event in which we work toward attaining genuine freedom to be vulnerable and to create healthy relations with others. This would encompass any number of social functions (prom to funeral) that conjure any number of emotions (elation to despair). Take, for example, the death of a loved one.

As we dress for the person's memorial services, we may feel sad and physically and emotionally weighed down by our loss. These emotions may cause us to put less effort into our dress. Perhaps we won't style our hair the usual way. We purposely may wear dark colors. We adorn ourselves in these ways to signify our grief. While the death of a loved one could cause all sorts of stressors, including financial worries and concerns for those left behind, our dress is not necessarily a sign of the bad stress or the anxiety that makes us want to hide our neediness with others. On the contrary, our funeral garb is a perfect example of an embrace of our vulnerability, a time when we are not afraid to show that we are dependent on others or to admit that relationships do, in fact, matter. In this case, what we wear and why we wear it are good in that they reflect our love of and honor for the deceased, including our complicated history of being needy and dependent on them.

Keeping with the notion that our funeral garb could be one of those invitations to embrace our vulnerability—in other words, manifest as good stress—it is arguable that such clothing creates the possibility for us eventually to move on and be hopeful again. In the Jewish tradition, there is a part of the funeral ritual during which members of the immediate family rend or tear their garments as a symbol of their grief. This is an instance of the good stress of dress, not because the death of the loved one is positive, but because this expression of vulnerability is cathartic and potentially transformative, moving the mourners to be hopeful for a brighter future.

Hope for the Here and Now. Certainly, hope is an important theme in the Christian imagination. I already have alluded to being baptized in the clothes of Christ as a symbolic ritual in which one is set on a trajectory of following Jesus' footsteps, all the while being supported with the care and concern of the larger Christian community. And in several of the examples offered in this chapter, including that of the Black church, the journey of Christian discipleship is sustained through dress by a commitment to and hope for salvation in the world to come. When we talk about the everyday practice of dress, however, the notion of hope needs to be nuanced a bit, for it is far too easy to conflate the theological idea and practice of hope with the *eschaton*, meaning the end-time, or what some like to call heaven. This is not necessarily wrong for Christians; in fact, it is an orthodox reading of hope. Yet if the whole intention of this book is to understand our ordinary day-to-day activities as invitations to meet God, then we cannot focus solely on hope for the afterlife.

It is worth returning to New Testament scripture to get a handle on the connections among what we wear, why we wear it, and what Christians believe about salvation in the here and now and the hereafter. Both of Paul's letters to the Corinthians emphasize this link between the end-time and dress in an effort to underscore how fleeting is the importance of day-to-day trivialities. In fact, the ordinary practice of clothing is used as a literary device to emphasize the importance of the resurrection of the body and the kingdom of God: "For this perishable body must put on [clothe itself with] imperishability, and this mortal body must put on immortality" (1 Corinthians 15:53); "[F]or in this tent, we groan, longing to be clothed with our heavenly dwelling—if indeed, when we have taken it off we will not be found naked" (2 Corinthians 5:2-3). These verses use clothing as way to argue that followers of Jesus are called to perform a certain way of being—one oriented toward God and eternity.

An important thread in Christian tradition and history, these sorts of texts certainly strive toward what I have been proposing: a spirituality of dress based on hope for a better world and a life-giving community. However, in our day and age, the danger of these texts is that they spiritualize dress too much. They could give rise to the perception that the here and now does not matter, fostering dualistic beliefs that are antagonistic to the world and the body. In an age of globalization, with consumerism proliferating throughout the world, electronic communication dominating our interpersonal relations, and virtual reality redefining our sense of being, it is fair to say that we are already alienated far too much from the value of embodied being. Spiritualizing clothing or any other embodied practice does nothing to retrieve the virtue of embodied vulnerability.

For those who want to get more comfortable with and even embrace the exposure of embodied being, another way of reading these Pauline texts is to emphasize hope in the here and now, not just in the hereafter. Christians might profess that we are all created in God's image and then through baptism and a life of discipleship are clothed in a fashion that orients us toward God and life-giving community, both here on earth and in what comes next. Put another way, being created with a certain dress—that is, in a sacred adornment of the image of God—sets us on a path that may reach impossible heights both in this world and in the world to come.

A God Complex? By now, it probably is apparent that part of the good stress of our daily dress practices is the way we exhibit hope for a better us and a better world. Christians have a particular way of speaking of the call to transcend ourselves in terms of being created in the "image of God." We read in the first chapter of the first book of the Bible, "So God created humankind in his image, in the image of God he created them; male and female he created them" (Genesis 1:27). While scholars understand this text in varied ways, one can say confidently that a core belief of Christian faith is that human beings are created with a gift from God, with the spiritual adornment chosen by God, one that reflects God's goodness, generosity, and interest in others. Being created in the image of God means having the look of God, or perhaps the imprint of the divine within us—a force that liberates us from our false sense of self, the closed self to which Vanier alludes, to a sense of self in which we are open, exposed, and vulnerable to being in genuine give-and-take relationships with others.

> In an age of globalization, with consumerism proliferating throughout the world, electronic communication dominating our interpersonal relations, and virtual reality redefining our sense of being, it is fair to say that we are already alienated far too much from the value of embodied being.

While receiving the gift of this image is flattering, it may at times feel more like a curse. We may think we are like God in that we assume we can have total control and are capable of perfection. Returning to the work of Niebuhr, one could make the claim that this is a fundamental paradox that human beings confront: being created in the image of God and being finite, having glorious promise and being constrained by mortality. This stress can be good, particularly when we draw on this anxiety to stretch ourselves emotionally, yet it also can spiral into a phenomenon of what I like to call the "god complex." We tend to say someone has a "god complex" when we want to disparage the person's actions, when we think the person has taken his or her sense of self too far and has no recognition of his or her limits or the needs of others— when we find the person conceited, egotistical, and self-involved. This is the bad stress related to being human and manifests in our dress practices, as we will see later in this chapter. For now, it might be worth revisiting Genesis and finding some good in the god complex, especially if what we mean by "god complex" is being magnanimous, creative, sacrificial, and so on.

The negative aspects of the god complex are tempered by the alternative image for humanity we find in Genesis 2, one in which humans are understood to be vulnerable, needy, and best when they are in relationship. When Christians read, "It is not good that the man should be alone" (Genesis 2:18), they are confirmed in their dependence on others and even encouraged to find solace in companionship. This story is often read as an oppressive and sexist narrative, in that the woman is made second and is the man's helper. It could also be read as a story about someone so lonely and incomplete that he needs another to bring authenticity to his life. This alternative reading of Genesis 2:18 emphasizes a God who endorses the human capacity for earthly love and friendship. Moreover, the second chapter of Genesis ends with these words: "the man and his wife were both naked, and were not ashamed" (Genesis 2:25). This statement points to the theological truth that being exposed in all our imperfections and neediness is part of the human condition and God's divine plan, and it corroborates Vanier's position that vulnerability is a normative dimension of humanity.

Bad Stress

Not everyone experiences the "what to wear" question with anticipation, creativity, and hope to live and reflect the image of God. Very few of us can muster the wherewithal to embrace the neediness and nakedness of the human condition. Many individuals, myself included, go all out to cover up neediness by attempting to look right and achieve the elusive goal of being in control and perfect. Feeling out of control, powerless, and less than God, we dress in an effort to shield ourselves from the emotional, psychological, and spiritual stress caused by our own or another's negative judgments about our human frailties.

There are reasons for this defensive response. Everywhere we look, vulnerability and limits are defamed, especially in consumerist cultures that seem to work and profit on the notion that limits need to be overcome. I like to refer to this as the "just do it!" mentality, memorialized by Michael Jordan in Nike advertising where he is pictured jumping with the ball to great heights, a sign of his dedication to greatness and his ability to overcome limits. In the midst of global capitalism, it is easy to be led into the predicament of wanting to be more than one can be as a creature—to have it all and then some. Overcoming limits is part of our cultural commerce. The media trade in this commerce by advertising the ability to overcome finitude and creatureliness through vitamins and steroids, age-defying makeup and cosmetic surgery, and cleansers and lotions.

While popular brands and products speak to our desire to transcend our limits and achieve what some perceive as perfection, they can also cause what I have been calling "bad stress" in that the hope they promise quickly turns into despair when we cannot achieve the goals of the brand. Even with those running shoes, we are still imperfect. Even with Botox treatments, we are still aging. Even if we shower three times a day with the latest cleansers, we are still needy. Theologically speaking, Niebuhr considers this situation to be a result of a fundamental aspect of the human condition, what he calls an "essential homelessness of the human spirit," in which we are always bound by creaturely existence but oriented otherwise and/or beyond.[11] That homelessness is unsettling and leads to our insecurity in which we do everything to cover up. This psychic and spiritual homelessness prevents us from embracing finitude as a gift from God for life-giving relationships with others.

> Overcoming limits is part of our cultural commerce. The media trade in this commerce by advertising the ability to overcome finitude and creatureliness through vitamins and steroids, age-defying makeup and cosmetic surgery, and cleansers and lotions.

This compulsion to hide our weaknesses goes beyond our consumption of specific articles of clothing, cosmetics, and so on to encompass the stories we tell regarding gender and vulnerability. *Big girls don't cry. Boys don't cry. Stop being codependent. You're so needy.* How many of us have been told these words or uttered these words ourselves? Our everyday sayings socialize, if not police, children into masking their fears, vulnerabilities, frailties, and weaknesses. We tend to glorify people who push through at all costs, including athletes who compete when injured to the point of hurting themselves further. These are the stories of bad stress that dominate our lives, often leading us into patterns of brokenness with God and others.

A Cosmological Time-Out. Christian stories are a resource for navigating this homelessness of the spirit that impels us to experience bad stress and push ourselves beyond healthy human limits. For instance, Genesis 3 is profoundly a story about the importance of being attentive to boundaries and of not succumbing to the negative effects of the god complex. The scriptural passage opens with God giving the first human beings anything they could want in a beautiful locale, except they are not to eat from the fruit of one tree. As many are aware, the narrative heats up as Eve submits to the serpent's temptations. Both she and Adam trespass against God's wishes and their human limits by eating the fruit from the forbidden tree, perhaps succumbing to what Niebuhr means when he speaks about the essential homelessness of the spirit.

This story moves me to empathize with all of us who are struggling to embrace our limits and vulnerability. It would be hard to resist the possibility of not dying, having my eyes opened, and being "like God, knowing good and evil" (Genesis 3:5), as promised by the crafty serpent. After all, Christians are taught to believe that humans are created in the image of God, so this is the next step, right? Many of us today meet the figurative serpent in the form of tempting advertisements that promise youth and beauty. I will look younger if I just use this or that face cream, and I will look thinner if I just buy this or that diet product.

Individuals and communities experience "the fall" over and over on a daily basis.

What is so interesting for this discussion is that after Adam and Eve eat (which is in and of itself a profoundly human activity of vulnerability), they feel compelled to dress: "So when the woman saw that the tree was good for food, and that it was a delight for the eyes, and that the tree was to be desired to make one wise, she took of its fruit and ate; and she also gave some to her husband, who was with her, and he ate. Then the eyes of both were opened, and they knew that they were naked; and they sewed fig leaves together and made loincloths for themselves" (Genesis 3:6-7). This passage is often read as a moment of shame, but another way of interpreting it is that, at that moment after eating, they are faced with their vulnerability, and it makes them uncomfortable. The problem is not nakedness; it is feeling bad about being naked. Analogously, the desire to be like God is not a bad thing; on the contrary, the challenge arises in accepting limits and creatively transforming the anxiety that being human generates. Perhaps we can read Genesis 3 less as a story about God punishing humans for not knowing their place and more as one that teaches about experiencing the negative consequences of vulnerability when creatures fail to realize their limits. That experience creates a cycle of covering up, which manifests in patterns of brokenness in our lives. These negative patterns eat away at our most cherished relationships by destroying our ability to accept and love ourselves and others in all our finitude.

The Impact of Bad Stress on Freedom. However one approaches Genesis 3 and its implications for Christians, we have seen already from the discussion of Vanier's work that worrying about our vulnerability impairs our freedom. Moreover, for a spirituality of dress to emerge, we must reenvision freedom in light of our vulnerabilities. In embracing our limits, even in how we approach something as ordinary and mundane as our dress, a more life-giving sense of freedom emerges, one in which we are thoughtful about and responsible for our interconnections with others locally and globally. Niebuhr writes about the relationship between anxiety and freedom quite poetically:

"Anxiety, as a permanent concomitant of freedom, is thus both the source of creativity and a temptation to sin. It is the condition of the sailor, climbing the mast (to use a metaphor), with the abyss of the waves beneath him and the 'crow's nest' above him. He is anxious about both the end toward which he strives and the abyss of nothingness into which he may fall."[12] Like Niebuhr's sailor, all of us and especially Christians are called to be reflective about how our anxiety affects our capacity for freedom, as well as to be thoughtful about how our anxiety limits the freedom of others. To be sure, we can never understand freedom as pure agency, because every thought we have of it is encoded and shaped by our feelings and needs, as well as by the needs of others. I remember learning this early

> Anxiety, as a permanent concomitant of freedom, is thus both the source of creativity and a temptation to sin. It is the condition of the sailor, climbing the mast (to use a simile), with the abyss of the waves beneath him and the "crow's nest" above him. He is anxious about the end toward which he strives and the abyss of nothingness into which he may fall.
>
> *Reinhold Niebuhr*

on as a divinity student and reading Roger Haight's work on sin and grace. An important Catholic thinker of our time, Haight explains that "there is no pure freedom," as "each individual person is both free and unfree, free and determined."[13] Emotions, including anxiety, are one of the dimensions of existence that affect our freedom. Realizing this allows us to make ethical decisions about what to wear and why we wear it. Fears about not being good enough could prevent us from trying new styles or could coerce us into adorning ourselves with certain products. We have to be vigilant about these effects if we want to have maximum engagement—freedom—in our lives.

Nevertheless, we cannot perform or enact a new sense of freedom alone. There is a whole global industry of capitalism, rife with designers, producers, manufacturers, and advertisers that influence what we wear and why we wear it. Are we truly free when we have been socialized from an early age to dress a certain way to be feminine or masculine? Are we really free when we have limited resources to acquire the clothing necessary to function in our schools or jobs? Are we really free when we want to buy shoes for our children and are paralyzed by not knowing where in China those shoes were made, who made them, and under what conditions?

To be sure, clothing ourselves is not a clear-cut process, and when we pause to think about it, our dress reveals how we are living out our anxieties in the best and worst of ways with limited resources as the negative patterns are cemented through social structures, including family, peer groups, industry, and the cult of celebrity. Struggling against negative patterns is not easy, and when we are faced with the challenge, the most radical solution may seem to be to overturn global capitalist social structures. However, for the ordinary person who is struggling to survive economically or emotionally, this may seem a bit daunting. Some might also ponder where any of us would be without these global capitalist structures. After all, these structures enable many of us to have clothes and other resources necessary for everyday life, so getting beyond capitalism does not seem like the easiest or most appropriate response to our anxieties.

As this book unfolds, I am hoping we can find ways to struggle against the bad stress and negative patterns in concrete ways, moving toward an acknowledgment of and commitment to what is sometimes referred to as "implicated resistance."[14] In working toward overcoming negative patterns related to what we wear and why we wear it, "[p]ersons of good faith do not stop being educated, stop being affluent, or stop bearing the particular privileged racial or ethnic system granted to them by the unjust system in which they live."[15] On the contrary, they imagine creative ways of transforming society as they live in their social locations. Implicated resistance allows for some to work against injustice on behalf of others in the midst of struggling with their own privilege. The anxiety that humans experience in being created finite and being created in God's image can spur wonder and personal and collective genius in all of us, regardless of our social contexts, to push ourselves to make a better world. Again, freedom is always "semiautonomous," and in addition to it being complicated by one's social status, there is a tendency to use freedom for personal gain.[16] This shadow side manifests when we use our freedom wittingly or unwittingly at the expense of others, when we adorn ourselves for our own achievement yet hurt other creatures in the process.[17] Seeing our interconnectedness and embracing our dependence on others is a good strategy for avoiding the shadow side of freedom.

This is a difficult point to get across, especially since many are conditioned by a sense of freedom for self and unbridled individualism. Thinking about my freedom in relation to that of another was never really part of my worldview, especially when I was growing up. I can recall that whenever anyone questioned my choices or complained about what I was doing, I would righteously and glibly state, "It's a free country!" I am not sure how I got that notion, but am worried that while I do not consciously say it or think it as an adult, my adornment practices today say the same thing. As I negotiate my human frailty through my dress, at times I implicitly announce with that same indignation, "It's my right and my prerogative!" That needs to be questioned. If anyone, including me, purchases clothing from manufacturers that are violating child labor codes, then perhaps we need to reevaluate our exercise and sense of freedom. If anyone, including me, publicly or privately condemns members of a religious group for what they wear, then perhaps we need to reevaluate our exercise and sense of freedom. In thinking through a spirituality of dress, we would do well to embrace a semiautonomous sense of freedom, one that values being intricately connected to others and thus responsible for them. This question of freedom and choice pushes us toward a conversation about sin. In the next chapter, I explore how sin emerges not so much in choosing this or that particular outfit, but rather in not paying attention to our stories about what we wear and why we wear it.

2

the path to perfection
is the road to destruction

"First take the log out of your own eye, and then you will see clearly to take the speck out of your neighbor's eye."
Matthew 7:5

Some years back, my father underwent a number of consecutive cardiac surgeries, all in the aftermath of barely surviving a massive heart attack. His brave surgeons risked much in taking on his case, as many others had turned him down because his health was precarious and surviving surgery seemed extremely unlikely. Known for their skill and experience, his surgeons operated anyway, and he survived for roughly another ten years. Our family was beyond grateful for his physicians' heroism and care, yet we found ourselves wanting more. We worried about how "normal" his life would be and whether the doctors could help him further. Very simply, his lead surgeon replied, "The path to perfection is the road to the destruction."

I have never forgotten that statement, because it struck a chord deep in my being. All my life, I have been involved in an on-again, off-again relationship with the ideal of perfection. It has been a catch-me-if-you-can relationship, in which the desire for perfection was somehow more addictive than the object of perfection itself. Though obviously I never have achieved perfection in any aspect of my life, the elusiveness of perfection has been a driving force throughout the opera of my every day. For years, I was convinced that perfection equals a good life and that anything less than being perfect is a result of not trying hard enough and/or of my human failing. For me, being less than perfect amounted to the same as being sinful.

Even though, time and time again, my neat formula for happiness was proven wrong, I still believed it to be true. When I was in middle school, I worked on a science project that involved constructing a model of human teeth. I worked really hard on this project, which was eventually to be part of a community science fair. Each day after school, I would open the refrigerator, where I stored my clay models, and would shape them ever so slightly, attempting to improve on the project. One evening, I pushed too hard, and the teeth literally fell apart. Looking back, I can confirm that the path to perfection is indeed the road to destruction.

Recently, my son, at a mere six years old, demonstrated that he had a better understanding than me of the dangers of wanting and needing to be perfect. When my four-year-old daughter was playing with her friend, my son overheard the other young girl criticize his sister for not coloring inside the lines. I could hardly hold in my overwhelming pride when he interrupted their conversation, arguing, "Perfection is impossible; people color in all different ways." He even added, in his righteous tone, that their "need for perfection is a problem." I see my son applying that understanding to the way his sister idolizes princesses. For my son, princesses are not real, because they are perfect. For my son, the qualities that define reality, meaning creaturely existence, are finitude, imperfection, and limits.

Several weeks later, however, my pride in my young sage gave way to sadness and guilt when he came home from school upset because he couldn't run the fastest. What had happened to his appreciation for human limits? When did he begin seeing imperfection as sinful, instead of a fact of his being part of what we call the human race? Had I passed on this distorted sense of what it means to be human? In the face of all these confusing queries, it was my turn to teach him that the path to perfection is the road to destruction. Even though we should try to improve our skills or qualities, at a certain point we may hit our limit, and that is OK. We have done our best.

This chapter explores the connections between our struggles with the idea of perfection and our lived stories about what we wear and why we wear it. My aim is to underscore moments in our everyday practices of dress in which we conflate imperfection with being sinful, as well as moments in which we ignore the sinful patterns about clothing we pass on to those around us. I hope to show that self-care and improvement through our adornment practices are not destructive on their own. Rather, it is when these efforts push us down the slippery slope into needing to look perfect or like the norm that they have the potential to project us into relationships and patterns of brokenness. This decline is evidenced in not feeling free to look otherwise than the norm, in feeling self-loathing, or even in bullying others who do not reflect the norms of dress, whatever they may be. Effort to achieve the elusive goal of perfection may also lead us into economic, physical, emotional, and perhaps spiritual debt.

Who Am I to Judge?

For years, speaking about sin has made me feel uncomfortable, so much so that I tended to avoid the conversation altogether. That is a hard call to make, especially since I teach theology. However, I stayed strong. After all, in a global world, where most of us are well attuned to the existence of varying cultures and a diversity of meanings and values that inform particular ways of life, it becomes nearly impossible to judge an individual or group's actions as wrong unless they verge on violating basic human rights. Even in those situations, "judging" can seem parochial and paternalistic. I am not just speaking from my personal perspective here, as I also get this cue from my students, who are reluctant to pass judgment on this or that individual or group because, in the words of my students, "We have never walked in their shoes." With their voices in my head, I get nervous when judgment is conflated with condemnation—in other words, when we call people or their actions sinful.

There is another reason I want to sidestep the *sin* word: a lot of the time, blame for problems falls on the same individuals and groups—namely, women and the marginalized. Eve's generosity (that is a tongue-in-cheek way of saying she freely offered Adam the fruit) jettisoned her and all the countless others into the categories of sinners, tempters, ignorant, and so on. Throughout the Christian tradition, women's bodies are imagined to be the devil's playground, a view that has led to despising women and seeing them as ontologically deficient. This misogynist legacy makes me hesitant to cast the first stone. Of course, I do realize and want to name that there is pain and suffering in the world, and that human beings are often implicated in that reality. Even so, because the category of sin has been used to demonize some more than others, I want to steer clear of it.

For Christians, however, forestalling conversation about sin is nearly impossible. And perhaps precisely because of the worry that judgment equals condemnation, we are called to return to the notion of sin and complicate it. Just judgment can neither be quick nor easy. Rather, as Bernard Lonergan puts it, judgment is only plausible "if there are no further pertinent questions."[1] Coming to any conclusion about what is a sin and

> In a consumerist global culture, in the hyped-up world of celebrity and computer-enhanced supermodels, and in a culture that some thinkers categorize as narcissistic, perfectionism manifests uniquely as the sin of our time.

who is a sinner cannot be premature; instead, it must be the result of careful reflection on the motives and needs of all the parties involved. When understood this way, some Christians may become less wary of broaching the topic of sin and brokenness. Serene Jones, who is a Protestant feminist theologian and the president of Union Theological Seminary in the City of New York, once and for all helped me realize that Christians cannot avoid the question of sin. She wrote that it is necessary to engage in "serious reflection on the depth to which persons can 'fall' in their brokenness and their participation in the breaking of others."[2]

So how does one begin to talk about sin and clothing without demonizing others or avoiding one's own implication in brokenness? It might help to make explicit the connections between sin and dress at the same time as we are vigilant about not blaming this or that group, since we usually are socialized from a young age into destructive patterns of dress. Growing up with an unhealthy and oppressive clothing practice does not legitimize it; rather, it provides a context for how to break out of that practice. It might help to make this more concrete. When thinking about how some people are practically mutilated from too much plastic surgery, it is all too easy to blame celebrities such as Heidi Montag and the late Michael Jackson for taking things too far—for having too many surgeries and setting poor examples for our youth. Similarly, when speaking about the exorbitant debt in which many people flounder today, it is all too easy to blame the want-to-be rich and to complain that they are ignorant and greedy. These sorts of gross stigmatizations of others are dangerous and misleading. Individuals do not act alone and are always enmeshed in complex situations and social institutions. We are always semiautonomous. Before calling someone or some dress practice sinful, we have to ask a couple of important questions: How did we get here? And what constraints on individuals coerce them into dressing in certain ways and not others?

In addition to blaming the same people all the time and ignoring how social pressures and structures might foster sin, there is another complexity to our discussion of sin and dress: making "hubris" a bad word in all circumstances. Jewish feminist theologian Judith Plaskow, in an early work titled *Sex, Sin and Grace*, urges us to gain an appreciation of the gender dynamics influencing understandings of sin, cautioning us not to conceptualize sin only in terms of pride.[3] This complicates our conversation, because if my premise is that many of us are struggling with perfectionism, a kind of hubris is associated with that desire. Nevertheless, for many women, according to Plaskow, pride is something they have been deprived of developing. Conditioned to be subservient to others in a male-dominated culture—and, I would add, in a white supremacist culture—some marginalized individuals and groups need to procure of bit of pride to become fully free and genuinely human. So when we talk about the sin of perfectionism, it is important to note that sin might manifest differently, depending on exactly which individuals and groups we are considering.

Perfectionism: The Eighth Deadly Sin?

From the early church forward, Christians have believed there are certain acts that destroy who we are and our capacity for charity. These mortal sins, at times referred to as the seven deadly sins, include wrath, greed, laziness, pride, lust, envy, and gluttony. In this section, I somewhat playfully and somewhat seriously suggest that we might think of perfectionism as the eighth deadly sin. To be sure, the unchecked drive to be perfect and godlike overlaps with greed, gluttony, and of course, pride, but in a consumerist global culture, in the hyped-up world of celebrity and computer-enhanced supermodels, and in a culture that some thinkers categorize as narcissistic, perfectionism manifests uniquely as the sin of our time.

It is somewhat awkward to propose that perfectionism is sinful, particularly when spiritual perfection is an important component of Christian life. From an early age, Christian leaders, educators, and caregivers teach children to practice their faith, to struggle against temptations, and to "press on" toward the goal of salvation (Philippians 3:12-14). The gospel story about Jesus' temptation in the wilderness, after he was alone for forty days with no food, offers a powerful example for believers to remain steadfast on the quest for perfection. The lives of the saints replicate Jesus' desert experience; in particular, Athanasius's *St. Antony of the Desert* concretizes the importance of perfecting one's soul through rigorous disciplines of bodily denial, including fasting and isolation.[4] For many mainstream Christians, the extreme mortification practices upheld by the narratives of the desert fathers are a thing of the past. Instead, fasting today is often limited to holy days as a reminder of one's devotion to God and the commitment to Christian discipleship. Still, there is a thread in the tradition that upholds extreme practices of bodily denial as a way to spiritual perfection, and those potentially damaging practices are the ones that need to be questioned both in Christian communities and in secular life.

> Perfectionism is the voice of the oppressor, the enemy of the people. It will keep you cramped and insane your whole life.
>
> *Anne Lamott*

Anne Lamott captures the more toxic and damaging effects of perfectionism in her inspirational work *Bird by Bird: Some Instructions on Writing and Life*. She writes, "Perfectionism is the voice of the oppressor, the enemy of the people. It will keep you cramped and insane your whole life . . . [and] is based on the obsessive belief that if you run carefully enough, hitting each stepping-stone just right, you won't have to die."[5] There is a paradox to perfectionism in that it promises immortality, but you practically have to kill yourself to obtain it. Just think of how multiple plastic surgeries take their toll on the human body, or how extreme dieting and weight training including steroid use harm one's health. Testing cosmetics in the lab poses harmful effects to animals. The path to perfection is the road to destruction.

Also poignant is Lamott's implicit critique of how perfectionism impedes human freedom. Christians believe first and foremost that God creates humans to be free, social, and with a sacred end. Perfectionism restricts our freedom to be creative, imaginative, and open to genuine relationships based on vulnerability. Lamott's words make plain what most of us know intuitively, that perfection is an illusion and death is certain. Reinhold Niebuhr puts the challenge in theological terms: "The evil in man is a consequence of his inevitable though not necessary unwillingness to acknowledge his dependence, to accept his finiteness and to admit his insecurity, an unwillingness which involves him in the vicious circle of accentuating the insecurity from which he seeks escape."[6]

Can Christians learn something of their "unwillingness" to embrace the human condition and vulnerability through careful reflection on their dress? What is the upshot of refusing to see through the veil of invulnerability we hide behind throughout our lives? These are difficult questions for even the most socially conscious among us. Perhaps the language of "veiling" provides an entrée into understanding how clothing functions as a cover for human imperfection. Throughout history, human beings, especially women, have worn veils to hide, surprise, and be modest. Yet many veils are translucent; you can see through them. The same is true of the veil we wear to feed our insatiable desire for perfection. It tries desperately to hide our human nature—the good, the bad, and all that's in between—yet ultimately fails. In struggling to keep up this illusion and not reflecting on the wake of damage it creates, we sin. Niebuhr's words are far more powerful than mine: "All efforts to impress our fellowmen, our vanity, our display of power or of goodness must, therefore, be regarded as revelations of the fact that sin increases the insecurity of the self by veiling its weakness with veils which may be torn aside. The self is afraid of being discovered in its nakedness behind these veils, and of being recognized as the author of the veiling deceptions. Thus sin compounds the insecurity of nature with a fresh insecurity of spirit."[7] Interestingly, one implication of Niebuhr's theology is that the fear of being realized as human is what keeps us from becoming fully human.

A way out of this illusion is simply to start seeing or, more than that, *paying attention.* Already I mentioned Lonergan's thought that making a judgment is not always a bad thing, but actually is an important step in human cognition and development—one that can only manifest with being attentive, intelligent, reasonable, and responsible relative to the matter. For Lonergan, refusal to pay attention is problematic, even sinful, if we use it as a denial of our humanity. It is not that we are purposefully inattentive, but for any number of reasons, some more conscious than others, most of us at one time or another refuse to really engage in knowing and being. The sin that Lonergan is concerned about is that of scotoma, which means blindness or a blind spot. This is not the physical manifestation of being unable to see, but of a refusal to see, of not being present and paying attention.

When applied to the issue of clothing, living as Jesus did may ask us to commit to being attentive to and evaluating the stories we tell and live by about our dress. Are they life-giving? Are they death-dealing? We need to acknowledge our stories about what we wear and why we wear it, not in guilt or self-hatred, but with knowledge that all narratives are complicated and prickly. We might look at the way we metaphorically veil ourselves instead of demonizing those who literally veil themselves, including those Muslim women who are constantly under sur*veil*-lance both from those in their culture and those outside their culture. We all are veiling in one way or another, and I am suggesting that we pause and think through our adornment practices and begin to reflect on which patterns of dress inspire freedom and which restrict freedom.

This takes work. It is more than chronicling the story of a young girl who badgers her parents to get her ears or some other body part pierced, and on the day of the piercing feels freedom. It is also thinking through how that perceived freedom might cause more problems and constraints on her freedom down the road. Stephanie Paulsell comments on what it takes to keep up the piercing, questioning whether that process really respects freedom or is just more gender work.[8] There are more or less extreme cases of dress restricting one's freedom. Pierced ears are benign in comparison to female circumcision or what some call genital mutilation. Another extreme case is foot binding. These are instances where scholars have argued that adornment has been manipulated as a way to control and suppress people's freedom and human dignity. Many reading this book might be far removed from these practices, but wherever we live and however we have been raised, to a greater or lesser degree, we participate in patterns of dress that constrain our capacity to be fully human, and sometimes we hand those patterns down to those around us.

The Trouble with Hand-Me-Downs

It is not unusual for Christians to speak about sin as being inherited. While some have maintained that this negative inheritance is passed onto others through the sex act, here I wish to suggest that we pass on sin through our destructive social norms. Sure, we are born with freedom, but many of the patterns we inherit about what it means to be a man or a woman or a human being, and many of the accidentals of our life story—including where we were born, who our parents are, and what religion, race, ethnicity, and gender we belong to—affect our capacity to enact that freedom. These inheritances may not make us or break us, but they definitely affect us. Christians believe that we are called to work to transform any patterns that cause suffering into life-giving ones, and to work on behalf of all those that suffer. Thinking about sin this way thwarts any move to condemn particular individuals or groups and allows us to conceptualize that sin emerges from a whole set of social assumptions and structures we have inherited, some of which are really oppressive to ourselves and others. It follows that the brokenness that comes from our clothing rituals does not usually originate

> All efforts to impress our fellowmen, our vanity, our display of power or of goodness must, therefore, be regarded as revelations of the fact that sin increases the insecurity of the self by veiling its weakness with veils which may be torn aside. The self is afraid of being discovered in its nakedness behind these veils, and of being recognized as the author of the veiling deceptions.
>
> *Reinhold Niebuhr*

with one person, but rather is a reflection of all the death-dealing values that have been handed down to us through our social institutions, including our families, schools, churches, laws, media, and so on.

My students appreciate this explanation of sin as inherited because they agree that we are born into a world with inequitable and unjust social structures and damaged relationships and systems. Even so, it is difficult for them to talk about the other side of that inheritance—namely, about the obligation to maintain it and, if the inheritance is damaging, to change it. Christian discipleship takes at its starting point the gospels through which Jesus is portrayed as critiquing the social problems of his time in an effort to change them. Following in his footsteps, Christians are called to acknowledge and transform the unjust social patterns of our time, including racism, sexism, homophobia, global poverty, and environmental degradation. Whatever gets handed down to us, especially the negative social patterns, must be grappled with in order to prevent brokenness in future generations. If we do not do something to acknowledge and change them, then we risk continuing to be part of the problem and handing down damaging patterns to those we love.

Girls Wear Pink and Boys Wear Blue. As a mother of two young children, I often find myself thinking about the patterns I am passing on to them, the hand-me-downs that stir ambivalence and, even worse, negativity. From the moment children are born, they are thrust on a trajectory of pink or blue, with little room for mixing and moving between them. Of course, gender is not just about colors, and depending on one's culture and context, gender performance extends to what is socially acceptable in specific articles of clothing, jewelry, cosmetics, hair and nail products, body cuttings, and so on. Taking note of daily dress practices quickly reveals to me how gendering unfolds in the most mundane of everyday practices, even for those of us who are vigilant about gender bias.

My preschool daughter takes great interest in my dress, watching as I adorn myself before I go to work. As I style my hair, apply makeup, and put on jewelry, she asks to do the same. When I am honest with myself, I have to admit I experience a strange sense of pleasure from her wanting to be like me, so much so that I comply with her wishes. I give her my brush, lipstick, and blush, and before long, this tender moment collapses. Smeared lipstick and a broken mirror on my bedroom floor—this is a snapshot of my conflict over what it takes to become a woman through clothing, and of my being implicated in the process. I begin to ask the questions I want to avoid: What exactly am I handing down to her? A story about what it means to be human? A life of being looked at and judged? How can I teach a four-year-old that no one's hair, makeup, and clothing can compare with the images of women that are digitally stretched, altered, and air-brushed? This is another mirror moment, but instead of me standing in front of the mirror, she is in front of me, and neither of us has the tools to deal adequately with the ambivalence of our reflections.

What does a life of being looked at actually entail? John Berger in the classic text *Ways of Seeing* pinpoints the extent to which girls and women are socialized into monitoring themselves: "A woman must continually watch herself. She is almost continually accompanied by her own image of herself. Whilst she is walking across a room or whilst she is weeping at the death of her father, she can scarcely avoid envisaging herself walking or weeping. From her earliest childhood, she has been taught and persuaded to survey herself continually."[9] Most disturbing about Berger's comments is the argument that women spend so much energy not only performing for others, but also judging their performance as they perform. They are actor, director, and critic all in one. Clothing aids in their performance. Even being naked is a type of performance, because it carries meaning and tells a story. According to this perspective, we are always performing, giving people what they want or at least what we think we want—the ideal image of a girl or of a boy, regardless of how disconnected that is from one's "true" experience or desire.

Some gender theorists liken the self-destructive and violent quality of gender regimens to being incarcerated, driving home the fact that certain clothing practices restrict our freedom and creativity. For example, Elizabeth Grosz in *Volatile Bodies* claims that "violence is demonstrable in social institutions of correction . . . marked by implements such as handcuffs." She then proceeds to compare that to what women and men have to go through to keep up their stories of femininity and masculinity. She explains: "Less openly violent but no less coercive are the inscriptions of cultural and personal values, norms . . . [through] stilettos, bras, hair sprays [and so on]."[10]

From where do these lessons on how to dress like a man or a woman originate? How far back can we trace our inheritance? For Christians, scripture and tradition detail rules related to gender and clothing. For instance, in Deuteronomy, there are clear restrictions on gender crossing through dress: "A woman shall not wear a man's apparel, nor shall a man put on a woman's garment; for whoever does such things is abhorrent to the LORD your God" (Deuteronomy 22:5). And in the New Testament, Paul writes about the importance of hair coverings for women (1 Corinthians 11:1-16).

In the early church, one only needs to look at Tertullian's "On the Apparel of Women" to understand how sin was thought of in relation to one's adherence to gender roles through dress.[11] In its most innocuous form, Tertullian's work valorizes modesty for both men and women, claiming that all Christians should dress in a way that resists the excess of consumption and wealth. This is not shocking, as Christian scripture maintains the need for modesty in dress. For example, in the New Testament we read, "Women should dress themselves modestly and decently in suitable clothing, not with their hair braided, or with gold, pearls, or expensive clothes, but with good works, as is proper for women who profess reverence for God. Let women learn in silence with full submission" (1 Timothy 2:9-11) and also, "[Wives,] do not adorn yourselves outwardly by braiding your hair, and by wearing gold ornaments or fine clothing; rather let your adornment be the inner self with the lasting beauty of a gentle and quiet spirit, which is very precious in God's sight"

> A woman must continually watch herself. She is almost continually accompanied by her own image of herself. Whilst she is walking across a room or whilst she is weeping at the death of her father, she can scarcely avoid envisaging herself walking or weeping. From her earliest childhood, she has been taught and persuaded to survey herself continually.
>
> *John Berger*

(1 Peter 3:3-4). Interestingly, this text elaborates to say that women should "adorn themselves by accepting the authority of their husbands" (1 Peter 3:5). However, men also are encouraged to show humility with their dress: "In the same way, you [men] who are younger must accept the authority of the elders. And all of you must clothe yourselves with humility in your dealings with one another, for 'God opposes the proud, but gives grace to the humble'" (1 Peter 5:5). Both genders are called to be humble, which in and of itself is not terribly off-putting to Christians, since humility is a hallmark of discipleship and in many ways a much-needed corrective to today's culture of economic excess and now collapse.

It is important to note that a call for modesty reflecting thoughtfulness about one's clothing and how it relates to others is different from a call for modesty that is really an excuse for one individual or group to control and dominate another. Tertullian's work verges on this latter problem when he shifts from touting modesty to demonizing women who go against their "natural" appearance. For Tertullian, that which is "plastered on" is the "devil's work." This sounds strangely familiar to a sentiment that surfaces today when women are encouraged to look a certain way through articles of clothing, makeup, and jewelry yet are ridiculed if they go too far. Women are pressured into being thin and looking young, and for the most part this is the norm. In some cases, however, women are labeled as becoming extreme in their actions. For instance, some female celebrities are practically publicly humiliated for their looks, with media probing into their life and assuming they have an eating disorder or body image disorder. While researching these body disorders is certainly valuable to saving lives, what I am pointing to here is the voyeuristic and blaming tone of these public accusations. There seems to be little room for compassion in the media coverage. Similarly, in her book in this series on the daily practice of shopping, Michelle A. Gonzalez insightfully notes how women are often in a double bind when it comes to shopping and fashion: they often are pressured into dressing a certain way but then typed as "vain" if they focus too much on their looks.[12]

While girls and women from all cultures and creeds are particularly tormented by norms and surveillance, boys and men carry similar burdens. It has been shocking for me to experience the dress pressures for boys through my son's eyes. In somewhat of a paradox, as he grows and experiences a widening social circle, his choices for how to be masculine narrow. Every time he chooses a shirt or a backpack, he is coerced into avoiding "feminine" colors. If he doesn't like black, blue, or green, I as his parent am faced with a similar choice. Do I suggest he go along with norms because of my own fears and projections about what he may or may not be subjected to in the school corridors, or do I leave him be and let the chips fall where they may? Parents want their children to be free and creative yet don't want to make them pariahs. In these moments, the hand-me-downs we offer our loved ones about what we wear and why we wear it undeniably influence their becoming human.

> For Tertullian, that which is "plastered on" is the "devil's work."

The question of when parents ought to intervene becomes even more pressing in the case of intersex children, babies who are born with ambiguous genitalia. Expansive literature cites the agony that parents go through as they address the question of gender assignment and the rights of the child. These children and their parents face inordinate pressure to conform to a sex, for gender ambiguity brings all sorts of negative and uncontainable emotions. In the past, many parents were coerced into having their infant children undergo sex reassignment surgery in order to avoid any gender ambiguity and confusion about identity as they got older. Nevertheless, in many cases, identity confusion does not disappear after the surgery. Clearly, there is a lot we do not know on the matter. Instead of being silent, we could alleviate some of the negative stressors in our lives by sharing stories of our anxiety about what we wear and why we wear it, including the stories of how we are dressed as boys and as girls. This is especially critical today, as bullying over gender and sexual orientation, at least anecdotally, seems to be escalating.

Christians are at a crossroads, called to model a new way of dress—one that is not afraid to discuss the issues about normativity and vulnerability, and one that imitates the healing and transformative power of the incarnation, so the same old destructive and divisive hand-me-downs are not passed on anymore. In taking on human existence, God not only sacralizes humanity, but also prioritizes all of these anxieties that permeate everyday human existence. They are front and center for God and for humanity. When read this way, taking the time to think about what we wear and why we wear it relative to freedom, dignity, and justice becomes a mode of Christian discipleship. Embracing our vulnerability and being present in our personal and political mirror moments has the potential to disrupt our mindless cycle of hand-me-downs and open us to new ways of dressing and being in relation to one another.

Do I Look Fat? How many times has someone uttered or heard this question? This is a common one among persons of the first world, who overconsume relative to others around the globe. Expectations and norms about body size and body shape are another bag of hand-me-downs that many of us can do without. While much of the common-sense conversation about weight loss and dieting centers around the plight of girls and women, researchers are discovering that boys and men struggle with their own body dysmorphic disorders (BDDs), diseases in which one has an ungrounded and unrealistic sense of what one looks like in terms of body size. While female BDD usually unfolds as thinking one is overweight when one is practically emaciated, male BDD usually manifests as thinking one is not ripped or big enough and feeling pressured to put on what some might consider "unnatural" and unhealthy muscle mass. In a provocative work entitled *The Adonis Complex*, clinicians explain that steroid use and obsessive weight training are fueling the male desire to be perfect, godlike even, leading to a condition called bigorexia.[13]

Many are familiar with two out of the three body disorders, anorexia, bulimia, and bigorexia. In anorexia, individuals starve, and in bulimia, they binge and purge. In the case of bigorexia, individuals, typically male, see themselves as too small physically and become obsessed with building muscle mass by spending an exorbitant amount of time and money at the gym working out. In addition, they often abuse steroids.

Categorizing body dysmorphic disorders as a type of dress may seem a bit of a stretch. Nonetheless, weight training, exercise, and dieting are all part of the process of clothing ourselves, of becoming who we are through putting on and taking off; instead of clothes, here we change body mass. Whereas much has been said about anorexia and bulimia, speaking about pressures on boys and men to get bigger is still taboo, and the media only drive this compulsion to be perfectly big. My favorite example of how the norms for male body size have changed in the past forty years is the evolution of G.I. Joe action figures. The torso and shoulders of the modern-day G.I. Joe have become so big they seem anatomically impossible. Another favorite of mine is the evolution of the Freddy Jones character from the *Scooby Doo* series. Over the past 40 years or so, he has gone from big to huge in terms of muscle mass. Although we are quite comfortable speaking about how supermodels' proportions are unrealistic and unhealthy, there continues to be very little discussion of bigorexia. Perhaps because men are not supposed to talk about or have feelings, or perhaps because some forms of steroid use are illegal, we have been relatively silent about this destructive pattern of dress.

Passing on these new norms about male body size expectations without any thought about the brokenness it leads to, including the disrupted relationships, the sick bodies, and so on, is a form of sin. And when we ignore the fact that boys and men also suffer from body image crises, we exacerbate the patterns of brokenness. I am amazed by the students in my Religion and the Body course who dare to share their struggles with bigorexia as well as those of their boyfriends and/or brothers. It becomes clear that in the case of body dysmorphic disorder, the desire for perfection not only destroys the individual in question, but also has a ripple effect, hurting others around them. Opening up to the simple reality that nobody is perfect allows us to heal these wounds and take an alternative road than one of destruction.

Outsourcing Sin

Sin never stays with the person who sins; it gets passed on to community, locally and globally. The Rev. Dr. Martin Luther King Jr. expressed this wisdom in his letter from a Birmingham jail, when he wrote, "Injustice anywhere is a threat to justice everywhere."[14] Other religious traditions also emphasize this ripple effect. In *Being Peace*, Thich Nhat Hanh, a Vietnamese Buddhist monk who has devoted his life to what he calls "engaged Buddhism," echoes this idea.[15] He explains that we all are dependent on and connected to one another. With these ideas in mind, here I suggest that sin is rarely containable and usually overflows onto others, even in the ordinary daily act of getting dressed. We need to think about this domino effect and even consider that without vigilance about what we wear and why we wear it, we run the risk of outsourcing sin, of letting it spread to other individuals and communities near and far.

Labels Matter. Probably the easiest way to start thinking about what we wear is to look at labels, those on our clothing, cosmetics, and so on. Labels matter, yet sometimes they tell only part of the story, and there are times when they just confuse us further. I have had my own trials with labels. My son loves sea creatures, and his favorite is the shark. His interest has opened me to think about the connections between humans and animals in ways I never had imagined. It is not as if we don't care for animals in society; in fact, some argue that we take better care of our pets than we do of children, especially underprivileged kids. Still, for most people, there is sense that animals have their place, an attitude that partially could be traced back to Christian beliefs that only humans are created with a soul. Whatever the reason, I want to suggest that the questions of sin and dress encompass the plight of all creatures. This is where my son's deep interest in sharks becomes relevant, as one of his greatest concerns is with the increasing numbers of sharks being mutilated for their fins, skins, liver oil, and so on. One estimate is that thirty-eight million sharks per year are fished, a rate that is not matched by shark births.[16] Not only does this place the shark population at risk; it degrades the entire aquatic ecosystem.

After we read our last shark book before my son's bedtime, I wash up and get ready to go to sleep myself. Looking into my aging eyes, I am reminded to apply eye cream. Something makes me look at the label. I get only part of the story. I am not really quite sure of the ingredients. Is shark liver oil one of them? Are sharks being slaughtered for my face cream? I am at an impasse. I feel I ought to go online and look up all the ingredients, but I don't have the time or energy. It is getting later, and I have an early meeting in the morning. I regret that there is no structured time or space in my daily routine to deal with these concerns. I fear that I am not alone, that many of us would like to know more about where, how, and at whose cost our favorite pieces of clothing are produced. Many feel powerless and paralyzed by looking at the label and not knowing anything more than it is made in this or that country. Our imaginations do the rest. Creating a space for a spirituality of dress allows me to talk about this paralysis and about how we cannot accomplish everything we want to or think we should in the day. In giving up on that idea, the idea of perfection and control, we create a moment for realizing how our sin and experience of brokenness are connected to the similar experiences of others.

Concern about the use and abuse of animals for cosmetics and clothing was probably most popularized by the group PETA (People for the Ethical Treatment of Animals). While PETA's tactics have been important for getting people's attention (most notably when PETA activists have thrown animal blood on individuals wearing fur in public), we need to pause and move beyond the blame game. No one is free from the problem of not knowing or being blind to what we wear and why we wear it. If we push the skin cream example a bit, we can trace complexities of brokenness further. It is easy to blame the workers who catch and kill the sharks, but perhaps their freedom is restricted too and they are reduced to this in order to feed their families. This is where the language of outsourcing falls apart, because it creates a fictive distance between the producer and the consumer. There is no *in and out*, no *here and there*, no *us and them*. We are all embroiled in complex "social arrangements" that influence who we are and how we choose to dress as witness to that identity.[17]

Sin is not merely a personal "yes" or "no" to wearing leather at the expense of animals or to buying running shoes at the expense of children's exploited bodies, although those are very critical personal choices. Nonetheless, with those decisions comes the realization that our response to them is influenced by patterns, institutions, and stories that ground our lives. Part of dealing with the anxiety about dress is admitting the ambiguity of those choices, a reality that is revealed to us by living in a global consumer society. Since boundaries among all the parties involved are unclear and at times porous, instead of blaming this or that individual or group, we need to think about how we are all implicated in these patterns through our adornment practices.

When it comes to the college students I meet, labels matter to them in any number of ways. Some want to be fashionable, some want economic justice, and some want to be eco-friendly. Some want any combination of these three. When they delve into their own stories about their dress, they quickly understand how sin exists in *not* seeing the impact of one's practices on the individual level, and then how sin goes global when their individual decisions about clothing hurt others, humans and animals. Students also speak about powerlessness, about wanting to become knowledgeable about where their clothes originate from and how they can transform their negative dress practices. When imagining a spirituality of dress, we are opened to ask these sorts of questions and express our concerns and anxieties, even if we don't have any quick and easy answers. We are compelled to research sweatshops and to find alternatives to them. We are invited to speak about global consumer cultures in nuanced ways, not just saying consumerism is the devil or that it is a fact of life. Perhaps we can learn more about human vulnerability and neediness from engagement with these important issues.

Rewriting the Script on Consumerism. I am one of the first ones to worry about greed. Living in the United States, many of us find it easy to get swept up into the frenzy of consumption and easily find ourselves in debt over homes, cars, food, and clothes. Advertisements for the latest shoes and hair and cosmetics are everywhere we turn. Sometimes our bodies even become walking advertisements. Think of clothing that displays Gap or Nike logos. Sometimes people are even paid to advertise by adorning themselves in certain ways. My favorite example is a woman from California who was paid to shave her hair and wear a temporary tattoo that advertised Air New Zealand on the back of her bald head. She was what they call a "cranial billboard."[18] In the midst of all this marketing madness, many of us encounter peers who think they never have enough and are oblivious to the privilege and responsibility of living in what some call the first world. Even worse is meeting children who imitate the adults around them, always wanting more and more, confusing wants with needs. Children are the future; sadly, many are brainwashed from an early age to believe that things will bring them happiness. Then, when things don't make them happy, they are taught to blame industry and corporations. The blame game doesn't end there, as certain groups of people, including women, often are targeted as the most egregious and thoughtless consumers.

With all this swirling in my head, I want to say—sort of joking and sort of seriously—that consumerism is the devil. However, that tells only part of the story. It is easy to blame this corporation or a certain group of women, but that denies how we are all implicated in this. Why do we blame them instead of thinking through all the rhetoric that puts us in this blame game in the first place? Also, we might consider that shopping for clothes and accessories can be life-giving. Some people find community through shopping. Gonzalez explains, "Shopping becomes leisure time, family time, a way to bond with friends."[19] Many of us have heard the phrase "retail therapy," referring to the experience of feeling better about life after shopping. Some may participate in the phenomenon of Black

Friday, where people do a ton of holiday shopping the day after Thanksgiving, leaving retailers potentially in the black. These activities, which tend to create community, are the same ones that are criticized in our broad-brush dismissal of the consumption of clothing as something negative.

Getting a new script about consumerism means taking note of what we are saying about what we need, what we want, and how our clothing practices intersect with these stories. Getting a new script might necessitate being honest about the following questions: How do we feel about our bodies? What kind of language do we use to describe them? Do we feel we need to control our bodies and embodied practices to fit into the human race? Is being overweight or dressed in secondhand clothes, according to commonsense knowledge, a sign of our being not good enough, even not fully human? I think these are terribly destructive notions and do not approve of them, but to move forward with a spirituality of dress, we might want to consider that these sorts of ideas circulate among our peers and, looking in the mirror, that we even may have thought them about ourselves.

> Is being overweight or dressed in secondhand clothes, according to commonsense knowledge, a sign of our being not good enough, and even not fully human?

Getting a new script about consumerism means not staying on one trajectory when speaking about capitalism or consumption—that it is all good or all bad, or that the ones who consume the most are the worst sinners of the bunch. It is easy to blame the individual for succumbing to societal pressures for wearing a veil or makeup, for getting too many piercings or not enough, for selling out to the plastic surgery route, and for running up debt on credit cards to have the latest fashions. Our brokenness is not generated in these isolated events, but rather through our inability to see how we are all struggling with being vulnerable and how we all are obligated to deal with our anxiety about our human condition.

The Roads Not Taken

In this chapter, we focused intently on sin and brokenness in terms of not paying attention to one's stories about dress. There are many other angles from which one could examine the relationship between clothing and sin. For example, as any high-fashion advertisement communicates, clothing signifies wealth and status, leading some to become greedy and envious of those who have better and more clothing than they have. Few can forget the story of Joseph's colorful coat in the book of Genesis. Joseph's garment, gifted to him by his father, made his other brothers sick with envy: "Now Israel loved Joseph more than any other of his children, because he was the son of his old age; and he had made him a long robe with sleeves. But when his brothers saw that their father loved him more than all his brothers, they hated him, and could not speak peacefully to him" (Genesis 37:3-4). We, too, experience jealously and envy when faced with someone who has been given more clothes or other things than us, and we struggle to understand and overcome those feelings before they fester into violence. Interestingly, such jealously occurs both in the local spaces, including the confines of our own home, and within the global panorama.

Conceivably, readers may have hoped for more on the status of sweatshops throughout the world and Christian responses to them. We could have investigated the "blood diamond" industry where these precious stones are mined to fuel oppressive regimes, leading to the exploitation and murders of countless innocent victims. The most obvious omission on the connection between clothing and sin could in all probability be the call for Christians to clothe the needy, since turning one's back on the poor and naked is sinful and negligent. While these ideas and others percolate throughout this book, and some will be discussed in more detail in the next few pages, here I have devoted most of the discussion to thinking about one small step individuals and groups can take toward having more life-giving mirror moments: being attentive to what we wear, why we wear it, and of course, the impact on others.

Each day before the mirror, we are invited to embrace being a creature with limits and needs, to love ourselves and those around us in all our imperfections. Dressing our children and buying our own clothes are opportunities to transform destructive hand-me-downs and consumer practices that we have inherited into moments of grace in which we say yes to God and the call to creaturely existence. Sin creeps in when we squander these sacramental occasions and refuse to be mindful of the effects of what we wear and why we wear it, as well as of how adorning ourselves to fit norms and be perfect damages others around us, including humans and animals near and far. To push against and convert these sinful patterns of not seeing into life-giving ones of seeing, we need to do a lot more than look at the labels. We must risk being thought of as vulnerable and get honest about how our "talk" about clothing can be just as damaging to others as the clothes we wear. A next step might be to embrace the work of Jesus Christ, homing in on the incarnation as a model for a new dress for humanity—one of nakedness and openness to the frailties of creaturely existence.

3

redeeming fashion

As God's chosen ones, holy and beloved, clothe yourselves with compassion, kindness, humility, meekness, and patience.

Colossians 3:12

How do we foster the good stress and overcome the bad stress in our day-to-day clothing? How can we transform sinful patterns of dress into redemptive ones? Perhaps the most important question, what's the incentive to do so? If this or that clothing practice mitigates our anxieties about the frailties of life, why change anything?

What I have attempted to demonstrate so far is that the rigorous adornment regimens that we participate in every day satisfy our need for control and desire for perfection only temporarily. Before long, our myth of control shatters, and we are back to the dressing room, trying to feel good about ourselves in the midst of all the anxieties that accompany the human condition. The incentive then is to find a new frame for our anxiety. We need to find ways not merely to look better, but even more than that, to live better. We need to redeem fashion.

Spiritual Resources for Embracing Vulnerability

Finding a new frame cannot happen unless we first acknowledge the problem, the figurative hand-me-downs that drag us and others down, the dress practices that limit human freedom and creativity and prevent Christian community and solidarity with others. We have already begun this by narrating the ways in which our clothing leads to positive and negative stress, as well as to individual and social sin. Now we can begin to imagine ways to transform the negative and destructive dress patterns into opportunities for grace—invitations to create more life-giving relationships with God and others.

••••••••••••••••••••••••••••••••••••

Before long, our myth of control shatters, and we are back to the dressing room, trying to feel good about ourselves in the midst of all the anxieties that accompany the human condition.

••••••••••••••••••••••••••••••••••••

The Christian tradition provides resources for embracing our humanity with grace rather than with resentment. As we push on toward constructing a spirituality of dress, it will help us if we not only look at the ways in which vulnerability is imagined in the first chapters of Genesis, but also widen our understanding of vulnerability. Being finite and limited—even needy—is not just something we have to tolerate as Christians; on the contrary, embracing it is part of our call to live in a way that honors Jesus' ministry, death, and resurrection. In moving from tolerance to embrace, we find resources in the tradition that encourage vulnerability as a way of being hospitable to and even in solidarity with others. Consider a few examples from the Old and New Testaments: God called the people of Israel to be thoughtful of how they act with strangers, since they themselves were estranged in exile. Mary, the mother of Jesus, gave her consent to enter into a precarious relationship with God as an unwed mother, and Joseph made a commitment to stand by her. The gospels often portray Jesus' ministry to the poor and outcast. Finally, throughout the Christian tradition and particularly in the work of Athanasius, we have theological claims that God became human as a way of offering relationship to humanity. All these elements in the tradition enliven Christians to imagine human frailty as a way to connect with others in open and genuine ways.

Empathy and the Exile Experience. Throughout scripture, there are frequent mandates from God to take care of the vulnerable, including widows, orphans, and strangers. In Exodus, the Israelites, who have faced suffering and abandonment at the hands of the pharaoh and others, are summoned by God to always remember those in similar precarious situations—to care for and protect them in this way: "You shall not oppress a resident alien; you know the heart of an alien, for you were all aliens in the land of Egypt" (Exodus 23:9). Likewise, in Leviticus, God commands the people, "When an alien resides with you in your land, you shall not oppress the alien. The alien who resides with you shall be to you as the citizen among you; you shall love the alien as yourself; for you were all aliens in the land of Egypt. I am the LORD your God" (Leviticus 19:33-34). These commands reveal a side of the divine that wants creation to acknowledge human frailty and neediness. Human beings are called to be empathetic to individuals and groups who are in need and who are dependent on others for compassion. This is more than a call to merely tolerate vulnerability, neediness, and even imperfection;

it is a sacred obligation to utilize those precise character-istics to create community and better the world. Refer-ring back to our discussion of Vanier in chapter 1 the notion that everyone at one point or another is in need—financially, emotionally, or spiritually—is in many ways freeing for humanity. In acknowledging our neediness, we are let off the hook and given permission to abandon our pretenses of being in control, all-powerful, superhuman, and perfect. What's more, our neediness is a tool by which we can create life-giving relationships with others.

"Hospitality" is one of those words that is used widely and in a myriad of ways. It tends to mean everything and nothing. Here what I mean by "hospitality" is the act of opening to the needs of the other, as well as acknowledging our own sense of dependence on others. At times referred to in terms of "charity," hospitality is a sense of welcoming the give-and-take of relationships. As such, being hospitable in the fullest sense is not a one-way street; it is a dynamic rela-tionship that is fluid and changing. We may find ourselves in need of another's help and resources, wanting for cloth-ing, food, shelter, or companionship. At other times, we may feel compelled to reveal to others that we are there to help, to be present in the relationship as an act of solidarity with the other. Whatever the dynamic, in addition to being hospitable to others, Christians are called to be in solidarity with those who are needy, standing by them and witness-ing to their frailty, not in a way that exploits them or makes them into a spectacle, but in an act of compassion and love.

While getting a handle on hospitality and solidarity in theory is somewhat straightforward, living these Chris-tian values in our daily dress is a bit more complicated. An obvious place to begin the conversation is to say that Christians are called to provide the needy with clothing, and in that way, Christians demonstrate openness to the need of others and willingness to stand with others in their vulnerability. In the Hebrew Scriptures, we read about the obligation to provide clothing for the needy (see Deuteronomy 10:18). Furthermore, in the Gospel of Matthew, Jesus implies that those worthy of his father's kingdom are those who clothe the naked and feed the hungry (see Matthew 25:35-38, 43). While these charitable acts are certainly part of a spirituality of dress, beyond this believers are called to understand how Christian values might unfold more basically as we begin to think about what we wear and why we wear it—specifically, if our clothing practices in and of themselves demonstrate a commitment to embracing the human condition, including all our anxieties about being needy and dependent on relationships with God and others.

Vulnerability and the Holy Family. All Christians honor Mary as the mother of Jesus and value her place in the tradition. Catholics have a special place for Mary in their imagination, as she is an icon for motherhood and compassion. She is the saint among saints, who sacrificed her good name to answer God's call to be faithful. In saying yes to God and being the mother of Jesus, she committed herself to a lifetime of relinquishment and grief. Michelangelo's *Pietà*, the famous Renaissance marble sculpture that sits in St. Peter's Basilica in Rome, immortalizes the sense that Mary occupies a pivotal place in Christian history and imagination as one who offered up herself and son for all of humanity. Michelangelo's Mary seems youthful and fragile, yet her bodily proportions appear larger than life. Whereas some may want to claim that she is holding her tortured son—a grown man—in her arms as one might cradle a baby with a warm, tight embrace, Michelangelo's Mary seems to offer her son out to the world.

Although there are many ways to read biblical narrative, art, and popular devotions related to Mary, here I want to argue that, for Christians, she is a role model for not merely accepting vulnerability, but embracing it. When Mary assents to the angel Gabriel in the Lukan gospel, "Here am I, the servant of the Lord; let it be with me according to your word" (Luke 1:38), her body and her story in one quick moment make room to accommodate another. She embraces vulnerability as a way to deepen relationships and commitments. Amid all the social pressure to conform to standards about marriage and sexuality, the gospels portray Mary as willing to be exposed and vulnerable in response to God's request. How Mary felt is practically impossible to know. We can say, however, that in saying yes to God and humanity, she succumbed to being out of control, vulnerable, and even chastised.

Christians committed to gender equality, including feminists and other liberationists, might want to resist glamorizing these self-giving aspects of Mary, especially since women in patriarchal societies always seem to be required to accommodate for others and are often the individuals responsible for hospitality. To be sure, Mary has been used, especially in Roman Catholic thought, to confine women to certain ideals about what it means to be a good mother. But when we take a closer look at Mary in the Christian story and really try to put ourselves in Mary's shoes, we realize that her life and her gesture of opening for others was much less than ideal. Mary's tough decision is often overlooked and taken for granted as something that was easy, especially since many artistic renditions of the annunciation (Gabriel's announcement that she will conceive Jesus) portray her as submissive and passive. But here I am trying to convey that being open to vulnerability is anything but passive. It is a painstaking process of letting go of control and reaching out in relationship to another. In saying yes to God, Mary exhibits that sort of fortitude—giving up on any ideal of a life that is perfect, nice, and neat. Hospitality for Mary is saying yes in the face of scorn and even being abandoned by her friends and family. Perhaps, in reimaging Mary's hospitality in this way, we can rehabilitate vulnerability in our everyday life, not as something we should avoid, but as the way we can most fully connect with God and others. Furthermore, as we continue working toward a spirituality of dress, we might envision our clothing practices as openings where we might express this new posture toward human exposure.

Mary was not alone in her radical embrace of vulnerability. When Christians speak about the Holy Family, they refer to Mary, Joseph, and Jesus. It might be helpful to look at Mary's partner, Joseph (often touted as Jesus' foster father), as another model in the tradition that embraces vulnerability as a way to connect with others. In the Matthean gospel, Joseph is confronted with a difficult decision about what to do in the face of Mary's pregnancy, and he "planned to dismiss her quietly" (Matthew 1:19). Before Joseph could do this, the angel Gabriel visited him in a dream and convinced him to stay with Mary. One might imagine that this posed a dilemma for Joseph, since after explaining that Mary was pregnant, he might have to divulge his dream and vision, causing further ridicule. One message Christians could take from this passage is the call to stand by the vulnerable in our world—unwed mothers, neglected children, and the needy in general.

Exposing oneself to ridicule is at times the cost of being in solidarity with others, and this vulnerability is precisely what is made sacred in images and snapshots of the Holy Family.

Jesus' Ministry. Keeping with the theme that the Christian tradition not only norms vulnerability but even makes it something to which we should aspire, it is fitting to look at Jesus' other-oriented actions during his ministry. As I have argued elsewhere, the gospels portray Jesus as someone who is consistently engaged with and transformed by the marginalized in society, including the sick, the poor, women, foreigners, the despised, and so on.[1] While he is oriented toward the plight of the other (the frail, the needy, the compromised, the imperfect, and so on), he does not try to fix them, but rather heals them. There is a difference between fixing and healing. The idea of healing highlights the emotional plight of those most vulnerable—their sadness, loneliness, anger, and fear of being abandoned. Jesus attends to those needs by bringing them into the community, by making them feel welcome, by being hospitable. He does not try to fix them so other people think they are normal; on the contrary, his touch and friendship make them feel accepted for who they are.

In addition to showing Jesus reaching out to others in his ministry, the Gospels portray Jesus as a messiah who asks his followers to do the same—that is, to show the same sort of openness to the other. In the Parable of the Great Dinner, Jesus asks his followers to demonstrate that same sort of other-oriented activity: "When you give a luncheon or a dinner, do not invite your friends or your brothers or your relatives or rich neighbors, in case they may invite you in return, and you would be repaid. But when you give a banquet, invite the poor, the crippled, the lame, and the blind. And you will be blessed, because they cannot repay you, for you will be repaid at the resurrection of the righteous" (Luke 14:12-14). While many Christians tend to domesticate these sorts of scriptural passages, conflating opening one's table to others with being kind and nice, it is refreshing to think about the truly shocking nature of what Jesus was doing and saying according to the gospels. Jesus, like Mary and Joseph before him, risks his own reputation to create community with the needy. Indeed, Jesus embraces his own vulnerability and risks exposure—being harassed, tortured, and killed—by entering into complicated relationships that challenge the social norms. Notice how vulnerability is embraced on multiple levels in that Jesus is reaching out directly to those who are the most vulnerable in society, and in doing so, he makes himself vulnerable to the wrath of others who fear his other-oriented activity.

Narratives about Jesus' becoming vulnerable for the needs of others are so central to Christian tradition and identity that they surface in other holy stories as well, including hagiographies, the biographies of the saints. For instance, Francis of Assisi is presented in the popular imagination as tending to the sick and the poor in medieval Europe. In a piece of modern hagiography on Francis, Donald Spoto writes, "With no money to give and no food to share—for he, too, was now reduced to begging—Francis knelt down and gave what he could: an embrace, a bit of comfort, a few sympathetic words. Francis would almost certainly have remembered the New Testament accounts in which Jesus healed a leper. 'Moved with pity, Jesus stretched out his hand and touched him,' which must have shocked bystanders as much as the cure itself did."[2]

Christians have integrated these radical traditions of literally reaching out to the vulnerable—the young, the poor, and the sick—incorporating them into sacramental rituals, including baptism and, for Catholics in particular, anointing the sick. In our everyday practices, many of us touch one another without thinking about the theological implications. When we hug a child who needs comforting or hold the hand of someone near death, we are being other-oriented and risking the safety of our comfort zones to expose ourselves for others. Being a follower of Jesus in light of these traditions means letting go of the pretense of being perfect and in control and jettisoning the idea that others need to be those things to be considered human and worthy of life. Living a life as Jesus did involves exposing oneself to the complicated, messy relations among all creatures of the world.

Beyond Jesus' other-oriented ministry, his embrace of vulnerability is for Christians memorialized in his dying on the cross—in a most humiliating and horrifying way—under the rule of the Roman empire, so others could have a better life. Through the cross, Jesus takes on the stories of many, including those who were most stigmatized at the time—women, the sick, and the outcast. Jesus does so as a witness to the oppression and suffering of others. He does not avoid death; he takes it on in solidarity with all of humanity. Moreover, Jesus does not experience a clean and peaceful death, but one of total exposure—so shocking that many of us wince just thinking about it. What's more, when Christians celebrate Jesus' resurrection on Easter, they too bear witness to the claim that vulnerability to the point of death births life. Far from being a condition that imprisons us, vulnerability is our greatest gift of freedom to relate to the needs and desires of others and create life-giving community with them.

Incarnation as Dress. In the introduction of this book, I referred to the work of Stephanie Paulsell, specifically her claim that we are all called into relationships of intimacy with the other, relationships in which we are denuded or made vulnerable. For Paulsell and many of the other voices I have surveyed in this book, vulnerability is a good thing. It propels us toward God and others; it is the basis for all relationships. The incarnation is a moment unlike any other that highlights the value of being creaturely and vulnerable. Indeed, in God becoming human, the frailties and anxieties of the human condition are made sacred. Here I want to elaborate on that claim and suggest that, in addition to the scriptural references we have considered (God calling the Israelites to care for strangers, gospel portrayals of Mary and Joseph embracing the liminality of human existence, and Jesus' risk-filled other-oriented activity), the Christian belief in the incarnation—that God became human through the flesh and blood person of Jesus Christ—is the ultimate example of the sacredness of embracing vulnerability.

The mere claim that God became human through the historical person of Jesus Christ fundamentally transforms how human beings think and feel about being vulnerable, frail, limited, and imperfect. Belief in the incarnation could be a catalyst for conversion, the beginning of approaching finitude with a sense of honor, awe, and vitality, rather than with a sense of being ashamed or compelled to change and/or cover up. At the very least, Christian witness to the incarnation gives humans permission to lay themselves bare and experience the freedom to be who they truly are. At the very most, the incarnation makes exposure for others a new goal for humanity—perhaps a more attainable one than perfection, and definitely a more gracious one, as it is embedded in hospitality to and solidarity with others.

If we want to apply classic religious themes here, it is fair to say that for Christians hospitality unfolds in God's offer of relationship in the incarnation, in being in union with human beings in all that they think and feel in their everyday life. As my students like to say, the Christian belief in the incarnation makes God relatable. Thinking more about the effects of the incarnation, one could make the claim that solidarity emerges in God bearing witness to the anxiety that accompanies human existence, to the wanting to be perfect and godlike. Christians proclaim every Sunday that, through the incarnation, God has walked in their shoes in birth, life, and death. God really knows what humanity is all about, to the point of embracing it. Consequently, Christians, having been called to imitate Christ, are compelled to embrace the frailties of humanity as an act of solidarity as well. Likewise, Christians are chosen to show hospitality to the other as God offers it to humanity. In a way, Christians might see that God, in becoming human, redesigns vulnerability as a new form of dress.

There are countless interpretations of the incarnation and just as many contributions to the study of incarnational theology, many of which developed centuries after Jesus' life. The Gospel of John says, "In the beginning was the Word, and the Word was with God, and the Word was God," and then the "Word became flesh and lived among us" (John 1:1, 14). This text is the foundation for imagining a God who becomes human and takes on the ordinary embodied experiences of men and women. Pertinent to our discussion, the language of "flesh" is stark and jarring, so much so that it resists any dualistic notion that human embodiment is an impediment to being like Jesus. Indeed, in this gospel, "flesh" becomes sacralized. This runs counter to the way many of us think about our bodies and embodied activities—that they are in need of control and discipline. I attempt to emphasize this embrace of embodied vulnerability in most of the classes I teach. Yet sometimes I feel as if I am lecturing on this point until I am blue in the face, as it clashes with what many of my students, and probably others, experience today, including ambivalent and negative feelings about their body and the messiness associated with embodied living.

The first few centuries after Jesus' death brought many shifts and developments in church doctrine, especially related to the meaning and reality of the incarnation. By the end of the fifth century, orthodox teaching reflected that "Jesus Christ is 'fully human and fully divine . . . one [person] . . . existing in two natures . . . without confusion, without change, without division, without separation'."[3] As definitive as this is, this formula did not fully squelch concerns about the right way to interpret the incarnation. To this very day, Christian leaders and scholars continue to debate the nature of the mysterious borders of humanity and divinity. There are many questions about the communication between the two natures.[4] How do the divine and human natures relate to one another? Does one dwell in the other? Are they side by side?[5] In contemporary theology on the incarnation, it is fascinating to see the constant theme in which the divine communicates and transforms the human nature, but not necessarily vice versa. Likewise, reading theology on the incarnation, one intuits that it is important to maintain that the divine nature overflows onto the human one, yet the human one does no such overflowing. There is the sense that we need to protect the divine nature so that human nature does not pollute it. This one-way communication seems to go against the spirit of the incarnation. As I understand it, the mystery of the incarnation has something to do with divinity and humanity being in a mysterious and unknowable relationship of intimacy. Both natures are present in the one person of Christ, and both are in a way hospitable to the other's needs. By being there in such intense proximity, the two natures witness to the good of the other and show solidarity to the other in a relationship of sacred vulnerability. In a world in which we are constantly feeling dragged away from the messiness and frailty of embodied being, through extreme cosmetic makeovers and digitally enhanced images, the incarnation invites us back to our humanity. In a world where we are socialized to think that being human is to be perfect and practically superhuman, the incarnation teaches us that it is OK to be human—in fact, that it is a gift because it intimately connects us with the divine.

A timeless and classic resource for thinking about what is at stake for humanity in God becoming human is Athanasius's *On the Incarnation*.[6] Athanasius was a bishop of Alexandria, Egypt, who lived and worked for the better part of the fourth century on Christology, which refers to the teachings about the person and work of Christ. Reading Athanasius's seminal work, one begins to grasp the Christian belief that human beings are recreated through Jesus' fleshly adornment. While Athanasius does not use the language of dress, he certainly suggests that God, in taking on the human form, transforms humanity.

As with the other-oriented activity in his earthy ministry, Jesus' incarnation brings transformation in the form of healing. In the face of human failing or what Athanasius calls "this dehumanizing of mankind," the incarnation revitalizes humanity.[7] According to Athanasius, God repackages Godself so that others can have new life: "He assumed a human body, in order that in it death might once and for all be destroyed, and that men might be renewed according to the Image."[8] In relation to our discussion, it is fitting to suggest that the incarnation is an offer of hospitality to humanity, an invitation to live a better and holier life. Moreover,

> In a world in which we are constantly feeling dragged away from the messiness and frailty of embodied being, through extreme cosmetic makeovers and digitally enhanced images, the incarnation invites us back to our humanity.

we could also say that God acts in solidarity with humanity by putting on and performing, in the most genuine sense possible, the human story. God tells a story of care and concern for creation, of hospitality and solidarity. Read this way, the incarnation is a form of dress—one of emotional, intellectual, and spiritual nakedness, one where life-giving relationships with others are the priority, making vulnerability the ideal fashion. While the style is one of a kind, it is an exemplar for others to wear. Put more concretely, God provides a model for Christians to embrace vulnerability as something good and valuable. According to Athanasius, God acts as a "good teacher with his pupils."[9]

An Incarnational Attitude. While humanity cannot replicate the incarnation, thinking about the incarnation as dress has the potential to foster in Christians an incarnational attitude, a sensibility that respects limits and embraces vulnerability—one that regards Jesus' embrace of the human condition as a legitimizing of it and, even more, a sacralizing of it. An incarnational attitude makes peace with one's imperfect body that neither a good outfit nor a face-lift can make immortal. An incarnational attitude resists self-hatred and dualism, and tries to overcome the bad stress that inevitably leads to our brokenness. An incarnational attitude struggles with the hand-me-downs we pass on to our family, friends, and even those we have never met. An incarnational attitude thinks about the stories people tell in their dress and tries to engender stories of openness to others and relationships of interdependence.

> The incarnation is a form of dress—one of emotional, intellectual, and spiritual nakedness, one where life-giving relationships with others are the priority, making vulnerability the ideal fashion.

What an incarnational attitude is not is an attitude that thinks about the specifics of what God wears—for example, fixating on Jesus' eye color or sex. Instead, an incarnational attitude embraces the spirit of this relationship of intense proximity, valorizing human vulnerability and frailty as sacred. When we reduce God's humanity in Jesus to his maleness, then we risk excluding women and others from the promise of new life. This goes against all our baptismal promises, in which we all are invited to put on the clothes of Christ. Rather than reducing the incarnation to a specific item of dress, it might be more life-giving if we conceptualize God's embrace of creaturely vulnerability more broadly, with a focus on his celebration of the human condition. Only then can all participate in the renewal that God initiates through Jesus Christ.

Christians believe finally that God, in becoming human, honors the predicament of finitude by taking it on. We are all chosen to respond to God's invitation, to honor God, by becoming naked ourselves. Christians hear this in Paul's letter to the Colossians, where he writes, "As God's chosen ones, holy and beloved, clothe yourselves with compassion, kindness, humility, meekness, and patience" (Colossians 3:12).

Some Christians may resist conceptualizing the incarnation in terms of dress, particularly since there is a heresy called Docetism, which is associated with claiming that Jesus only appeared human and was God masquerading in human form. They would certainly be right to be critical if what they mean by adornment is putting clothes on an object that connotes no meaning, like a blank slate or, better yet, a mannequin. However, throughout this book, I have argued the opposite—that clothing never amounts to dressing up what is naked. In fact, I have attempted to show that we are never really naked, if by the term we mean natural and untouched. Even naturalness is a form of dress in that it is context driven and conveys some sort of meaning and value depending on one's social world.

Getting Naked with Jesus

In *Nudity: A Cultural Anatomy*, Ruth Barcan develops the idea that nakedness is just another form of dress, one that "comes into being with the invention of clothing."[10] Like others who have written on issues of gender, race, and embodiment, Barcan claims that "the nude body is never naked, if naked means stripped of meaning, value, and political import."[11] It is not as if we are "blank" pages, slates, or scripts—that is, something void of meaning—and a new dress works to cover us.[12] It is more the case that we are constantly engaged in a process of negotiating who we are to the world through states of dress and undress. In their discussion of nakedness, many scholars attempt to show that being considered "natural," "normal," or "naked" is always a construct of a particular worldview. Consequently, all these labels refer to a form of dress in that they tell a story, revealing meanings and values of a specific way of life.

This is such an important point in the discussion of a spirituality of dress that it warrants further explanation. In a commonsense manner, the word *naked* might evoke thoughts of a person who is not wearing any clothes. It is fair to say, moreover, that some naked bodies are more culturally acceptable than others. What if a colleague shows up to work naked? People would consider that individual crazy, not normal or natural. The person's lack of clothes—his or her nakedness—is a sign of the person not conforming to social expectations, and the nakedness is anything but neutral or a blank slate. It is deviant dress. In contrast, babies without clothing do not signify deviance at all. Their dress tells the story of their cuteness, innocence, and precious vulnerability. Many of us have pictures of ourselves or our children running around our home naked. These examples are two ends on the spectrum of dress. Whatever

> Nakedness, according to Ruth Barcan, "comes into being with the invention of clothing."

the state of dress, being clothed, unclothed, and all the permutations in between signify something and tell some sort of story.

In constructing a spirituality of dress, Christians might want to consider the implications of nakedness not meaning an absence of content. In fact, being dressed in nakedness could represent a sacred type of being. Like newborn babies, Christians are called to embrace their vulnerability and the vulnerability of another—in effect, to get naked. This is, of course, a spiritualizing of the term *naked*, and later I will suggest ways that actual articles of clothing can be worn and still convey this nakedness. Yet for now, it is worth reflecting on whether Christian discipleship demands not only tolerating this nakedness but, more than that, cultivating lives of being emotionally exposed, vulnerable, and limited—in other words, being creatures. Nakedness calls us into relationship with others and grows out of the moments of good stress that make us hopeful about our future and the life-giving relationships in it.

Emmanuel Levinas, a significant Jewish thinker of the twentieth century, employs the terms *nudity* and *nakedness* as metaphors for illustrating how the need of another acts as an impetus for ethical relationships. The frail and vulnerable one who stands before us has the potential to denude us and undo all our pretenses about being in control, above it all, perfect, and godlike. Levinas writes, "The Other challenges and commands me through his nakedness, through his destitution. He challenges me from his humility and from his height."[13] For Levinas, the neediness of others in our lives has the potential to disarm us, and it is up to us to be hospitable to those others in need by revealing our own frailties and limits.

Levinasian theory has an abstract quality. If we want to make nakedness more concrete, it might help to return to a previous example. In response to the vignette I shared in the second chapter about my daughter appropriating my anxieties about beauty and image, getting naked might simply mean being honest and sharing one's ambivalent feelings about beauty and dress, even with a preschooler. As my daughter looks up at me with her innocent face, I am called to reveal my human frailties and show her ways to embrace them in her own life. It is really never too early to start the conversation, because from the beginning of their lives, children are getting messages from their peers and the media about what to wear and why to wear it. Children could benefit from a conversation or many conversations about what we wear and why we wear it. One does not have to be technical and mention Niebuhr or any other theorist per se; it is enough to begin talking to our sisters and brothers, sons and daughters, nieces and nephews, and students and friends. If we do not start talking soon about the stress of dress, we risk passing on the same old patterns and damaging hand-me-downs that may have made our own lives less beautiful.

Nakedness and the Christian Imagination. As already alluded to throughout this book, Christians are called to bear witness to the incarnation by being thoughtful about and committed to vulnerability in their adornment practices. Sharing stories is one aspect of nakedness, of being willing to let the walls come down and reveal one's anxieties about the limits of the human condition. This exposure can be cathartic, and Christians have a particular way of speaking about this letting-go-of-oneself that getting naked involves: the term *kenosis*. In its most general use, the term refers to emptying oneself for another, just as God does for humanity in the incarnation. In the next few pages, however, I will expand the notion of kenosis beyond emptying to mean making room for another creature and/or perspective, and taking on a new way of being.

In his letter to the Philippians, Paul writes, "Let the same be in you that was in Christ Jesus, who, though he was in the form of God, did not regard equality with God as something to be exploited, but emptied himself, taking the form of a slave, being born in human likeness. And being found in human form, he humbled himself and became obedient to the point of death—even death on a cross" (Philippians 2:5-8). This text, which is part of a hymn that was repeated in Christian worship during the early church, shows how so much of living like Jesus involves emptying oneself. I have been using the phrase *getting naked* not necessarily to be provocative, but more to highlight the risk involved in this sort of mentality. Also, as we will see later on in this chapter, the term *naked* is being used by other ethical movements—for example, the organic food movement—which can remind us that dress is like any other embodied practice in which Christians are called to be in right relationships with God and all others. In getting naked, Christians might consider how they can dress in a way that relinquishes all pretenses of being in control.

While most often thought of as emptying and relinquishing oneself for that of another, kenosis can also be understood as an overflowing of one nature to the other, or even curbing oneself to make room for another. When we read the term in any and all of these ways, we can see that God, in giving up the one story of divinity to take on two natures, divine and human, overflows in solidarity with humankind and shows hospitality for humanity by making room for the needs and wants of another. Humans are oriented toward these same accommodations in their everyday lives.

Nowhere are the spiritual connections among dress, nakedness, and living a life like that of Jesus more palpable than in the stories told about Francis, the late-twelfth-century mendicant who founded the Franciscan order. Well into his ministry, he was described as tending to the poor and sick, risking his reputation and bodily harm for the most vulnerable in his community. Before that, he lived a quite different and most extravagant lifestyle. He was the son of Peter Bernardone, an affluent Italian businessman who traded in fabrics throughout Europe. As his son, Francis reveled in a world of privilege and excess throughout most of his youth and into his adulthood. After failed attempts at finding greatness in military endeavors, the young man from Assisi experienced a conversion that compelled him give up his reckless, spendthrift ways and begin a life of asceticism. His family, first ashamed of his wild lifestyle and then even more upset about his new life of public commitment to the gospel, demanded that he change his ways and pay his debts. In a symbolic act in front of Bishop Guido and his father, Francis disrobed, creating a spectacle that cemented his commitment to a new life— one of nakedness. Spoto comments, "Nakedness was thus a powerful symbol of what Francis desired: freedom, like that of the naked newborn, without the burden of worldly goods or privileges, without the pleasures and responsibility of possessions and fine clothes."[14] While these written narratives are certainly provocative, paintings boldly capture the affective import of his getting naked. In a famous fresco in the upper basilica in Assisi, Italy, Francis is shown giving up his worldly clothing. This fresco (*Renunciation of Worldly Goods*, circa 1290), which is attributed to the medieval artist Giotto di Bondone, is a stunning example of how important kenosis is to Christian life. Wearing a tunic given to him by the bishop and his head surrounded by a halo, Giotto's Francis is portrayed as reaching up toward a hand in the sky, giving up his worldly desires for a greater calling—a life in which he could be in true communion with God and the world, humans and animals alike. Nakedness in this saintly story is not a blank slate or absence of content, but rather is a decision to be totally transformed by an embrace of one's vulnerability, frailty, and dependence on God and others. This kenotic event is about both giving up and taking on: Francis not only disrobes but also takes on a new form of dress—a new story of renewal and hope, which emerges from prayer, discipline, and getting naked for God and others.

> Like newborn babies, Christians are called to embrace their vulnerability and the vulnerability of another—in effect, to get naked.

Christians are called, even if analogously, to this type of kenotic nakedness that renews us and fills us up. As Vanier explains, we become human in letting go of our false self; however, in becoming naked, we do not return to any pristine state. Rather, in sharing our stories, we respond to a deep desire for transformation and open ourselves to grace-filled relationships. Nakedness represents a rebirth, a second chance, and hope for the here and now as well as the hereafter. Minding the trap that nakedness is about being a blank slate and that clothing is the writing on that slate, it might help to consider that nakedness and dress may not be opposites; rather, nakedness can be seen as a form of dress. Indeed, for Christians, nakedness is the most spiritual and sacramental adornment regimen in which we are called to participate.

There are many references to nakedness in the Christian imagination, but perhaps no narrative is better known than the nakedness we read about in Genesis 3. In this passage, readers are introduced to the classic story about Adam and Eve, as well as what is sometimes referred to as the fall of humanity and the beginning of original sin. After disobeying God's wishes and eating from the tree, the two garden dwellers become keenly aware of their vulnerability: "Then the eyes of both were opened, and they knew that they were naked; and they sewed fig leaves together and made loincloths for themselves" (Genesis 3:7). Anxious about their nakedness, they scramble to cover up, reducing clothes to an unfortunate consequence of their transgression, which made "clothes a sad necessity."[15] According to this widely held perspective, nakedness signifies ignorance, sin, pain, abandonment, punishment, and even death.

However, this interpretation need not be the dominant reading of nakedness or of Genesis 3. Antithetical to this traditional understanding, perhaps nakedness in the garden signifies the human race's realization that we all are in need of others and cannot act alone or contrary to the good of community without consequences. This is what I attempted to show earlier in the first chapter when I described Genesis 3 as a cosmological time-out. Adam and Eve are like many of us struggling to assert our autonomy in a social world that values agency and despises dependence. Nakedness in the garden is a realization of the deception of the myth of complete control, freedom, and power. Like babies born naked, dependent on others to care for and nurture them, we are naked spiritually, dependent on God and others to care for and nurture us. A rereading of Genesis 3 for me is not so much about the fall as it is about the painful acknowledgment of our limits and the fact that everything we do is influenced by others and affects others. Simply put, nakedness in Genesis 3 reminds us that we are absolutely dependent on others—on God, human beings, all the plants and animals of the earth, and so on.

With each of these snapshots of nakedness in mind, Christians are urged to answer the call to get naked—that is, to become vulnerable to the neediness of relationships with God and others, to open with a heightened receptivity to God's grace. In becoming flesh, God is not above, below, or around, but dwelling within creaturely existence, with an openness to the complexities of humanity. In the place and space that many of us are trying desperately to escape, mortality and the embodied rituals of everyday life, Christians are invited to find God. If believers are called to imitate Christ in their everyday lives, then they are called to embrace creaturely vulnerability with the same spirit as the one in which it is offered.

> In the place and space that many of us are trying desperately to escape, mortality and the embodied rituals of everyday life, Christians are invited to find God.

The Bottom Line. Everyday kenosis does not mean that everyone should dress plainly, wear burlap, or even stop trying to be beautiful, though questioning societal norms and expectations is part of a spirituality of dress. Moreover, everyday kenosis does not mean asking the somewhat glib question of *What would Jesus wear?* Beyond the fads of wearing necklace crosses and W.W.J.D. (What Would Jesus Do?) merchandise, we need to begin coordinating our adornment practices with Christian values by imagining our choices about dress as rituals of solidarity and hospitality.

When read this way, a spirituality of dress might actually mean *not* wearing a cross for a necklace in some contexts, as the cross has a complicated history. It is a violent symbol—one of death and stately power. Wearing a cross is not like wearing a red ribbon to show solidarity with those who have HIV/AIDS and to support research of the illness. It is potentially much more emotionally charged. The cross tells a deadly story of countless individuals under Roman occupation, a context in which someone who questioned the inequities of the empire and wanted to help those who were vulnerable and marginalized would be risking death. How many Christians really know that the cross is a symbol of imperial power, heralded by Emperor Constantine, and hence fraught with all sorts of political and religious overtones? How many really know that some individuals and groups feel uncomfortable around the cross because it is a reminder that, for almost two thousand years of Christian history, Jewish individuals and groups were wrongly held responsible for the death of Jesus, a Jewish man?

This is the type of kenosis we need when we talk about what we wear and why we wear it. We need to consider anxieties about not meeting the norms of our specific cultural context, of wanting to be perfect, and also about how specific Christian dress practices might hurt others to whom we are called to be hospitable and with whom we should experience solidarity. This sort of mindfulness and attentiveness can help us work through the scotomas that may be distorting our ability to see the real meaning of our dress and relationships. Simply put, everyday kenosis related to dress means becoming aware, cognizant, and knowledgeable about what we are wearing, why we are wearing it, and how our dress affects others.

Beginning to publicly tell stories about what we wear and why wear it is a small but important step in moving toward a spirituality of clothing. Christians know the power of stories, as Jesus according to the gospel writers was a master storyteller himself. While parables might not move us toward revealing our anxieties about human limits, honesty can. This is no easy task. Telling stories about our feelings or our clothing—never mind our feelings about our clothing—often attracts suspicion and even mockery, as both are conceptualized as touchy-feely topics that are unimportant relative to the big picture of life. Casual dismissal of these types of operatic, everyday stories is in all likelihood a strategy to avoid dealing with these issues because they require us to delve deep into our spiritual being. Dealing with these issues requires difficult questions about whether the way we are living is life-giving, and if so, to whom or to what we are giving life. If one is shamed into thinking these types of stories are insignificant, then one feels less comfortable discussing them and avoids this type of spiritual work.

> Wearing a cross is not like wearing a red ribbon to show solidarity with those who have HIV/AIDS and to support research of the illness.

To break out of cycles of decline and patterns of brokenness, we need to be courageous enough to tell these types of stories with all their intellectual, emotional, and spiritual rigor. We need to stand steady in the face of disparaging words—accusations that we are just being touchy-feely. And we need to be in solidarity with others when they muster the courage to tell their own stories, too. We must be prophets in a world caught up in a complex myriad of interconnected, destructive mirror moments, and we need to allow spaces for telling and listening to stories that emotionally and spiritually expose one another. Sin as scotoma is born from our choices to conceal our stories, to be locked up in our own private hell of our mirror moments. Transforming this sin cannot be accomplished through blame or guilt, as both have paralyzing effects. Rather, our freedom and creativity need to be ignited so we can reach out to others and be honest about who we are and, of course, what we wear and why we wear it. We need to create places to imagine new mirror moments, moments that are life-giving in their embrace of human frailty. This exposure is not empty of content, but rather is overwhelming and overflowing, like God's unknowable and unending love in commitment to humanity through the incarnation.

Making Vulnerability Fashionable

For Christians, there is little doubt that something happened in the incarnation. God opened up the way for everyday kenosis, for making human vulnerability fashionable. Aside from the praxis of storytelling, how might Christians embrace the vulnerability in their dress to the point of making vulnerability fashionable in ordinary life? As evocative as images and ideas related to Jesus' nakedness may be, it is not too strong to suggest that in global capitalist culture, many need to buy into the importance of embracing their sacred vulnerability in the first place, before they can transform the sinful patterns of consumption, debt, and exploitation that lead to brokenness in their lives.

One of my local grocery stores has a clever way of marketing its animal products. It refers to the meat processed with fewer hormones and with more attention to animal care as "naked." Meat packages are labeled Naked Chicken, Naked Beef, Naked Pork, and so on. These naked products are extremely popular because people are becoming more concerned about what they eat and why they eat it. This is not a new concern. For years now, thinkers and activists, including Peter Singer, Michael Pollan, and David Foster Wallace, have spurred our imagination on the connections between what we eat and why we eat it, between what's on our menu and the quality of life of the animals on that menu. Today it is not unusual to ask how the animals were treated or what they were fed. Telling stories about the unethical treatment of animals raised for food and the debilitating effects of pesticides and hormones on the foods we eat, and then creating *naked* products in order to address these justice concerns, is akin to what I am asking for in a spirituality of dress. Much as some shoppers have already begun to buy into the "naked" concept of organic food, we need to begin imagining "naked" moments in our adornment practices as events in which our commitment to Christian discipleship can be renewed and reshaped.

Buying into nakedness in any aspect of life does not have to be as crass as it may sound. Getting naked in our clothing practices does not mean vulnerability must be a fad or appealing to the lowest common denominator. Yet getting naked does need to become more popular; it has to be able to move many people in a new direction and into embracing a new sensibility. I am extremely suspicious of a "buy-in" mentality, as it makes me wonder about who is benefiting from others buying in, and whether the product being sold is just another unnecessary thing we are told we need in the midst of global capitalism. Gonzalez echoes this sentiment when she admits to finding the "connection between charity donations and consumerism in the United States to be especially disturbing" and questions the "need to buy in order to give."[16] I appreciate such critiques. A hermeneutic of suspicion is always a good idea, yet if it keeps one from being open to new ideas and from changing, then it could end up debilitating us. The question is how one can make vulnerability fashionable without selling out to market greed and exploitation. Is that even possible?

Going Grunge. In the mid-eighties, musicians developed a genre called grunge, an eclectic mix of punk and independent rock. Along with this fad, some individuals began applying the term *grunge* to a certain look, characterized by unkempt hair, sometimes a dirty appearance, and punk clothes. For some, grunge is just a mere cultural fad, with no real countercultural punch, meaning it did nothing to change the oppressive clothing practices into which many feel forced. In this sense, the grunge look was just another regimen.

My students tell me that this "dirty" style is still fashionable. In fact, one recalled a family member spending a lot of money to achieve this unkempt style. Perhaps even in spending money on it, this unkempt look is an act of resistance, of getting naked and critiquing the over-the-top adornment practices of consumer culture. Many individuals today do not consider themselves part of any grunge subculture yet still like to think of themselves as dressing comfortably—for example, by wearing sweat-pants and T-shirts. Students, people who work from home, and others resist the norms of dress through the simple act of dressing down. While I don't want to make more of being comfy than is warranted, there is something thought-provoking about everyday people saying no to the norms of fashion and consumer culture.

Just Dress. Scanning the clothing market, one sees major initiatives in creating naked forms of dress, from eco-friendly clothing to items produced in coopera-tives that benefit communities in developing countries. Even more mainstream are big corporations trying to sell their dress products in support of a justice issue. The (RED) campaign is quite successful at raising awareness and resources for underdeveloped African communi-ties.[17] Quoting from the campaign's website, we can see how (RED) uses capitalist logic for a just cause: "(RED) is a simple idea that transforms our incredible collective power as consumers into a financial force to help others in need." (RED) organizes top brands, including Apple, Gap, and Hallmark, to create (RED) products, in which up to half of the profit is funneled to HIV/AIDS programs. This is a big-business justice initiative, and part of me wants to reject it as inadequate because it is tied to consumer-ism. However, for many of my students, this type of pro-gram offers hope. Perhaps this is the students' best effort at this point in their lives of being attentive to what they wear and why they wear it. This just might be a first step in developing a spirituality of dress. So many of the students I encounter express that that while they know about the social and economic inequities of the world, they are so guilt-ridden by their knowledge that they feel powerless to do anything at all to correct the problems. "Buying into" these campaigns might be a place for them to start getting kenotic. To be sure, while these corporate initiatives should not be seen as getting one off the hook from being naked, they might be understood as one small step on the road to nakedness.

Another popularized "naked dress" campaign is the "One for One" initiative from TOMS Shoes. My students educated me about this movement, which is detailed at the TOMS Web site: "In 2006, American traveler Blake Mycoskie befriended children in Argentina and found they had no shoes to protect their feet. Wanting to help, he created TOMS, a company that would match every pair of shoes purchased with a pair of new shoes given to a child in need. One for One. Blake returned to Argentina with a group of family, friends and staff later that year with 10,000 pairs of shoes made possible by TOMS customers."[18] Students can relate to Mycoskie's feeling of wanting to help. They buy into the idea that each of their purchases will improve the lives of children in developing countries by enabling them to attend school, as well as to avoid injury when playing and working.

I ask students whether they believe that this movement is doing enough and whether it is a ploy to prey on privileged people who want to make some sort of difference. Is it just a way for people to feel good about themselves when they are buying stuff they may or may not need, and potentially running up debt? Many of the students respond by asking me, "What is so wrong with feeling good about oneself through dress?" The implication of my students' response is that as long as people are going to keep purchasing, they might as well consume in an ethically conscious manner. For my students, as for the naked-food movement, this is a worthwhile and just practice. I am becoming more and more convinced of my students' argument. It is OK to start here and move forward.

If this type of nakedness is not naked enough, another group to consider is SweatFree Communities, a campaign that seeks to support workers in sweatshops worldwide and transform the global economy to enact just practices.[19] Certainly there are other "just" clothing initiatives readily available to many of us. By considering these ordinary routes, it is not that I am giving up on hard-core nakedness; rather, I am admitting that living on the ground is complicated. For real change to take hold, we may need to let go of the idea that our dress can save the world and instead might imagine ourselves and our actions as vehicles of implicated resistance, whereby we work for justice in the midst of having privilege. Recall my previous example of feeling powerless in my relationship with my daughter to teach her any other way than how I was socialized, as well as the question of whether TOMS Shoes goes far enough to enact justice. With regard to both situations, one can say that we—especially those of us who are privileged—can and are called to negotiate alternatives to sin by acknowledging the anxiety of living between two worlds, the desire for transcendence and the reality of limitedness, and to create a space for conversation about how to dress with others in a way that embraces that ambivalent space.

It becomes clear that getting naked with Jesus involves two steps. The first is being honest about our limits and frailties and sharing stories about how we cover up our anxieties through our daily dress practices. The second involves demonstrating our commitment to a life of nakedness by seeking out clothing that reflects openness to all creatures and admits our dependence on them. We need to make nakedness something we aspire to, rather than merely tolerate, and our dress ought to reflect our aspirations. These two steps are interwoven with one another, and at times, we might become disoriented and tempted yet again by the eighth deadly sin—the allure of perfection, control, and even godliness. These are bumps along the road, and it helps to consider that embracing vulnerability and nakedness is not a one-time event. Rather, it is a winding, emotionally exhausting journey with many blind spots along the way. While getting naked with Jesus certainly takes emotional work, the pay-off could be huge in that we free ourselves up for some of the most authentic and life-giving relationships imaginable and perhaps some we could never have imagined before.

notes

Introduction

1. Mark C. Taylor, *Hiding* (Chicago: University of Chicago Press, 1997), 127.

2. Ibid., 129.

3. J. C. Flugel, *The Psychology of Clothes* (New York: International Universities Press, 1971), 34.

4. Bernard J. F. Lonergan, *The Lonergan Reader*, ed. Mark D. Morelli and Elizabeth Morelli (Toronto: University of Toronto Press, 1997), 116.

5. Stephanie Paulsell, *Honoring the Body: Meditations on a Christian Practice* (San Francisco: Jossey-Bass, 2002).

Chapter 1. Vulnerability and the Human Condition

1. Susan Wendell, *The Rejected Body: Feminist Philosophical Reflections on Disability* (New York: Routledge, 1996), 93–105.

2. Jean Vanier, *Becoming Human* (Mahwah, NJ: Paulist, 1998).

3. See preface in J. C. Flugel, *The Psychology of Clothes* (New York: International Universities Press, 1971).

4. Reinhold Niebuhr, *The Nature and Destiny of Man* (New York: Scribner, 1949).

5. Stephanie Paulsell, *Honoring the Body: Meditations on a Christian Practice* (San Francisco: Jossey-Bass, 2002), 59–60.

6. Karen Anijar, "Jewish Genes, Jewish Jeans: A Fashionable Body," in *Religion, Dress and the Body*, ed. Linda B. Arthur and Gabriella Lazardis, 181–200 (Oxford: Berg, 2000).

7. Ibid., 181.

8. M. Catherine Daly, "The *Paarda* Expression of *Hejaab* among Afghan Women in a Non-Muslim Community," in Arthur and Lazardis, *Religion, Dress and the Body*, 147–61.

9. Mark C. Taylor, *Hiding* (Chicago: University of Chicago Press, 1997), 123.

10. Gwendolyn S. O'Neal, "The African American Church, Its Sacred Cosmos and Dress," in Arthur and Lazardis, *Religion, Dress and the Body*, 117–34.

11. Niebuhr, *The Nature and Destiny of Man*, 14.

12. Ibid., 185.

13. Roger Haight, "Sin and Grace," in *Systematic Theology: Roman Catholic Perspectives*, 2nd ed., ed. Francis Schüssler Fiorenza and John P. Galvin (Minneapolis: Fortress Press, 2011), 394.

14. Serene Jones and Paul Lakeland, eds., *Constructive Theology: A Contemporary Approach to Classical Themes* (Minneapolis: Fortress Press, 2005), 150.

15. Ibid.

16. Haight, "Sin and Grace," 384.

17. Ibid.

Chapter 2. The Path to Perfection Is the Road to Destruction

1. Bernard J. F. Lonergan, *The Lonergan Reader*, ed. Mark D. Morelli and Elizabeth Morelli (Toronto: University of Toronto Press, 1997), 174.

2. Serene Jones, *Feminist Theory and Christian Theology: Cartographies of Grace* (Minneapolis: Fortress Press, 2000), 70.

3. Judith Plaskow, *Sex, Sin and Grace: Women's Experience and the Theologies of Reinhold Niebuhr and Paul Tillich* (Washington, DC: University Press of America, 1980).

4. Athanasius, *St. Antony of the Desert* (Rockford, IL: Tan, 1995).

5. Anne Lamott, *Bird by Bird: Some Instructions on Writing and Life* (New York: Anchor, 1995), 28.

6. Reinhold Niebuhr, *The Nature and Destiny of Man* (New York: Scribner, 1949), 150.

7. Ibid., 207.

8. Stephanie Paulsell, *Honoring the Body: Meditations on a Christian Practice* (San Francisco: Jossey-Bass, 2002), 66.

9. John Berger, *Ways of Seeing* (London: BBC/Penguin, 1972), 46.

10. Elizabeth Grosz, *Volatile Bodies: Toward a Corporeal Feminism* (Bloomington: Indiana University Press, 1994), 141–42.

11. Tertullian, "On the Apparel of Women," trans. S. Thelwall, from *Ante-Nicene Fathers* 4, ed. Alexander Roberts, James Donaldson, and A. Cleveland Coxe (Buffalo, NY: Christian Literature, 1885), rev. and ed. for New Advent by Kevin Knight, http://www.newadvent.org/fathers/0402.htm.

12. Michelle A. Gonzalez, *Shopping,* Compass: Christian Explorations of Daily Living (Minneapolis: Fortress Press, 2010), 24–25.

13. Harrison G. Pope, Katharine Phillips, and Roberto Olivardia, *The Adonis Complex: How to Identify, Treat, and Prevent Body Obsession in Men and Boys* (New York: Simon & Schuster, 2000).

14. Martin Luther King Jr., "Letter from a Birmingham Jail [King, Jr.]," April 16, 1963, African Studies Center, University of Pennsylvania, http://www.africa.upenn.edu/Articles_Gen/Letter_Birmingham.html.

15. Thich Nhat Hanh, *Being Peace*, ed. Arnold Kotler, with illustrations by Mayumi Oda (Berkeley, CA: Parallax, 1996).

16. Save Our Seas Foundation, "How Many Sharks Are Caught Each Year?" http://saveourseas.com/articles/how_many_sharks_are_caught_each_year.

17. Roger Haight, "Sin and Grace," in *Systematic Theology: Roman Catholic Perspectives*, 2nd ed., ed. Francis Schüssler Fiorenza and John P. Galvin (Minneapolis: Fortress Press, 2011), 399.

18. Andrew Adam Newman, "The Body as Billboard: Your Ad Here," *New York Times*, February 17, 2009, http://www.nytimes.com/2009/02/18/business/media/18adco.html.

19. Gonzalez, *Shopping*, 14.

Chapter 3. Redeeming Fashion

1. Michele Saracino, *Being about Borders: A Christian Anthropology of Difference* (Collegeville, MN: Liturgical, 2011).

2. Donald Spoto, *Reluctant Saint: The Life of Francis of Assisi* (New York: Viking Compass, 2002), 58.

3. As cited in Serene Jones and Paul Lakeland, eds., *Constructive Theology: A Contemporary Approach to Classical Themes* (Minneapolis: Fortress Press, 2005), 168.

4. For a survey of theological approaches to the incarnation and the "communication" that transpires between the divine and human natures, see Oliver Crisp, *Divinity and Humanity: The Incarnation Reconsidered* (Cambridge: Cambridge University Press, 2007).

5. For an interesting analysis of the idea of indwelling versus juxtaposition, see Joseph Cardinal Ratzinger (Pope Benedict XVI),

Behold the Pierced One: An Approach to a Spiritual Christology, trans. Graham Harrison (San Francisco: Ignatius, 1986).

6. Athanasius, *On the Incarnation*, with an introduction by C. S. Lewis, trans. and ed. A Religious of C.S.M.V. (Crestwood, NY: St. Vladimir's Seminary Press, 1998).

7. Ibid, 40.

8. Ibid., 41.

9. Ibid., 43.

10. Ruth Barcan, *Nudity: A Cultural Anatomy* (New York: Berg, 2004), 1.

11. Ibid, 9.

12. Elizabeth Grosz, *Volatile Bodies: Toward a Corporeal Feminism* (Bloomington: Indiana University Press, 1994), 156.

13. Emmanuel Levinas, "Transcendence and Height," in *Basic Philosophical Writings*, ed. Adriaan T. Peperzak, Simon Critchley, and Robert Bernasconi (Indianapolis: Indiana University Press, 1996), 17.

14. Spoto, *Reluctant Saint*, 55.

15. Barcan, *Nudity*, 54.

16. Michelle A. Gonzalez, *Shopping*, Compass: Christian Explorations of Daily Living (Minneapolis: Fortress Press, 2010), 83.

17. "About (Red)," http://www.joinred.com/aboutred.

18. TOMS Shoes, http://www.toms.com.

19. SweatFree Communities, "About Us," http://www.sweatfree.org/about_us.

suggestions for further reading

Arthur, Linda B., and Gabriella Lazardis, eds. *Religion, Dress and the Body*. Oxford: Berg, 2000.

Athanasius. *On the Incarnation*. Introduction by C. S. Lewis. Translated and edited by A Religious of C.S.M.V. Crestwood, NY: St. Vladimir's Seminary Press, 1998.

Barcan, Ruth. *Nudity: A Cultural Anatomy*. New York: Berg, 2004.

Berger, John. *Ways of Seeing*. London: BBC / Penguin, 1972.

Flugel, J. C. *The Psychology of Clothes*. New York: International Universities Press, 1971.

Goffman, Erving. *The Presentation of Self in Everyday Life*. New York: Doubleday, 1959.

Gonzalez, Michelle A. *Shopping*. Compass: Christian Explorations of Daily Living. Minneapolis: Fortress Press, 2010.

Grosz, Elizabeth. *Volatile Bodies: Toward a Corporeal Feminism*. Bloomington: Indiana University Press, 1994.

Hewitt, Kim. *Mutilating the Body: Identity in Blood and Ink*. Bowling Green, OH: Bowling Green State University Popular Press, 1997.

Paulsell, Stephanie. *Honoring the Body: Meditations on a Christian Practice*. San Francisco: Jossey-Bass, 2002.

Pope, Harrison G., Katharine Phillips, and Roberto Olivardia. *The Adonis Complex: How to Identify, Treat, and Prevent Body Obsession in Men and Boys*. New York: Simon & Schuster, 2000.

Taylor, Mark C. *Hiding*. Foreword by Jack Miles. Chicago: University of Chicago Press, 1997.

reader's guide

1. For a week, keep a clothing journal. Each day after you dress, write down your feelings about what you are wearing and why you are wearing it. If you experience negative emotions, try to imagine what needs to change for you to feel more positive.
2. With those closest to you, including friends and family, discuss where you learned what appropriate dress is. Evaluate whether or not those messages are life-giving.
3. Reflect on how you feel about being vulnerable and needing others. Then consider whether your dress embraces vulnerability or works to mask it.
4. On any given day, begin to imagine your clothing as a form of autobiography. Explore what your clothing communicates about you and your expectations of others.
5. Try to recall the first time you thought of the difference between masculine and feminine clothing. Discuss whether those memories are pleasant or unpleasant.
6. Think about the connection between your clothes and animals. What ethical obligation do Christians have with regard to choosing what they wear with

attentiveness to how animals were used in the production of their clothing?

7. In this book, dress is not limited to shirts, pants, and jackets, but rather encompasses body modification practices such as plastic surgery, weight training, piercing, and tattooing. How does including these practices in a definition of dress influence how you think about what you wear and why you wear it?

8. Think of the messages or "hand-me-downs" we pass on to our loved ones about what is normal and natural in terms of clothing. Which of these hand-me-downs are life-giving for you, and which are death-dealing?

9. Look at the labels on your clothing. What do they tell you about how your clothes are made? Would your patterns of dress change if you knew more about the people and production process behind the label? Why or why not?

10. Theorists suggest that nakedness is a form of dress. What do they mean by this, and do you agree with such an argument? Why or why not?

11. For Christians, risking personal safety so that others can feel safe is part of Jesus' message. What does it mean to risk personal safety in terms of dress? How does one begin to "get naked" with Jesus?

12. Are there fads in consumer culture that resonate with the Christian call to live in service for others? If so, are these fads truly spiritual, or are they just schemes to get the public to buy more stuff? How do we know?